RESISTANCE-FREE
RIDING

Resistance-Free Riding

* * *

RICHARD SHRAKE

* * *

Breakthrough

To Lee Ann, with all my love.
Thank you for organizing me
and our office.
I am forever grateful to you.

For information address:
Breakthrough Publications
Ossining, New York 10562

Designed by Jacques Chazaud
Printed in the United States of America
Library of Congress Catalog Card Number: 93-71632
ISBN: 0-914327-49-6

Contents

❀ ❀ ❀

PART TWO

Preface

❀ ❀ ❀

One of the most important facts that I have realized during my career as a horseman is that a good rider will help and improve a mediocre horse while a poor rider, even with the best knowledge and training, will hinder and hurt a good horse. This book has been written for that special breed of horseman and horsewoman who will never settle for less than they can be—and are committed to increasing the quality of their riding skills so that they can achieve 100 percent total harmony with their horse. No matter what level of riding you are at, the "five master keys" will become an enormous source of strength and insight, enabling you and your horse to become friends and partners, with unlimited opportunities.

As I look back on the time and dedication spent on this book, I am reminded of the triumphant center of a basketball team. The center takes the plan from his coach on the sideline into the game. Then, after great team effort and total harmony from each of his fellow players, he is passed the ball in the final seconds of play. He makes the dunk that wins the game. The crowd cheers and the center becomes the public hero. However, the center knows better than anyone else that the victory was a team effort. In the game of life there are many coaches and team players. My whole life I have been surrounded with these hidden heroes. It is hard to put on paper the admiration and feelings I have for the many family members and loyal friends and peers that have made this book a true team effort.

To my family: your love and support is my strength. Nothing is more important to me.

To the many trainers and riders who shaped so much of my

philosophy, strategies, and skills throughout my career: a special thank you for sharing your knowledge.

My special thanks goes to Jim Becker, Dianne Eppers, Larry Mahan, Gigi Skelly, Les Vogt, and Dave Whitaker, who have given me their enthusiastic support.

A big thank you to the many friends and horsemen and horse-women who have been so kind to send photos to use in this book: Al and Becky Dunning, Doug and Val Milholland, Les Vogt, Ronnie and Karen Richards, Cynthia and Red Cantleberry, Sharon Camarillo, Robert and Sue Ingersoll, and Garth and Brenda Brown.

To Jim Bordvedt: my special thanks. You are truly a profes-sional—the best photographer I know.

To the many talented horses that have made me look good over the years. Their unconditional obedience and acceptance of train-ing made it possible for me to build a reputation as a trainer.

To the many gifted students who have let me be a part of their lives. Whether I was standing at the back gate of a schooling show or at a World Championship, the pride in seeing you give 100 percent made me stand a little taller.

I am so grateful to the many people around the world who have invited me to hold one of our Resistance-Free Riding and Training seminars or clinics. It is your hard work and promotion that prepares the ground for the students who attend. And, of course, thank you to the many students who have attended our seminars and clinics. It is your courage and dedication to your horses that inspire me to do my best. I have learned from you and acknowledge you for your participation.

To the many tack stores that have carried our Resistance-Free Riding program for their customers. Your sensitivity to education is changing the horse industry.

I take my hat off and salute the following companies that have given their faith and support to our program: Purina Mills, Circle Y Saddlery, Bailey Hats, and Miller Harness.

To our Sunriver Community Christian Church. Your prayers and constant love have given our family the love and loyalty to balance our lives. Most of all I give credit for the gifts given to me by my creator, our Lord Jesus Christ.

RICHARD SHRAKE
Sunriver, Oregon

Foreword
by Jimmy Williams

❀ ❀ ❀

Having had the pleasure of knowing Richard Shrake for more years than I think he'd like to admit, it's an honor for me to write this foreword for his new book.

As you read about his accomplishments in the following pages, you will gain a feel for his lifelong dedication and commitment to the sport of good horsemanship. He is intelligent in numerous different fields, from western pleasure to reining to speed events, to mention just a few.

His knowledge and fondness for both people and horses shine through and expose his expertise. He enjoys passing it on to young and old, pleasure riders and show champions. His books and videos are excellent guides for anyone who wants to enjoy riding.

Richard is innovative, patient, personable, and an asset to the business. He describes how he has expanded his horizons by traveling all over the world, broadening his training, riding, judging, and teaching abilities. Something can be learned from every new person you meet, or any new horse you ride. Richard explains this well, and if you use his resistance-free system, you will find it is the key to successful riding. He emphasizes relaxation, and how it holds hands with confidence, opening the doors to success.

His five master keys apply to all riding disciplines. By learning to use these tools, you will learn to ride off of your reflexes. Until a rider can do this, he or she is still in a mediocre phase of riding.

I've never read a more thorough explanation of what good riding is all about. Richard confirms in this book the aptness of my old saying, "It's what you learn after you think you know it all that counts."

Acknowledgments

❀ ❀ ❀

Unless otherwise listed below the photographs have been provided courtesy of Jim Bortvedt.

Page 2	Courtesy of Childress Photography
Page 12	Courtesy of Cynthia Cantleberry and Don Trout
Page 14	Courtesy of International Arabian Horse Association
Page 18	Courtesy of Ronnie and Karin Richards
Page 28	Courtesy of Team Penning USA
Page 35	Courtesy of Pony Association of America
Page 35	Courtesy of Pat Ingram
Page 45	Courtesy of the American Quarter Horse Association
Page 62	Courtesy of Les Vogt and Rick Osteen
Page 73	Courtesy of the American Quarter Horse Association
Page 74	Courtesy of the American Quarter Horse Association
Page 80	Courtesy of Doug and Val Milholland
Page 103	Courtesy of Al and Becky Dunning
Page 123	Courtesy of Garth and Brenda Brown
Page 131	Courtesy of the Appaloosa Horse Club
Page 133	Courtesy of Bobbie and Sue Ingersoll
Page 138	Courtesy of Team Penning USA
Page 146	Courtesy of the Appaloosa Horse Club
Page 148	Courtesy of Cynthia Cantleberry
Page 149	Courtesy of International Arabian Horse Assoc.
Page 156	Courtesy of Sharon Camarillo
Page 157	Courtesy of Brenda Allen
Page 164	Courtesy of the Appaloosa Horse Club
Page 168	Courtesy of the Appaloosa Horse Club
Page 171	Courtesy of the Appaloosa Horse Club
Page 172	Courtesy of the Appaloosa Horse Club

Introduction:

❀ ❀ ❀

How It All Began

One plus one equals one.

No, this isn't new math. It is good horsemanship. One horse and one rider, both resistance-free, equal one working unit, a relationship unique to horse and human. No other domestic animal has served man in so complete a manner, as servant, companion, and tool. In return we owe it to the horse to achieve as complete a relationship as we can, one in which complete communication becomes possible, and thus, complete trust.

Resistance-free horsemanship is a way to attain that total harmony in which rider and horse become one. The skill level of the rider plays a major role in how well the horse accepts its role in the relationship, that of being trained and used for its intended purpose. Because the rider's skill can make or break this relationship, it is important that each rider work hard to establish unity.

It is always being said that good riders are born, not made.

Richard Shrake

That certain elements of skill and ability that turn a good competitor into a star are impossible to learn.

Forget that.

Using the principles of resistance-free riding, you can greatly improve your riding skills. You may even be motivated to take your new abilities all the way to the top of your sport.

Competitive horsemanship has reached such a high level of difficulty that a rider needs every edge and advantage to excel; and one moment of resistance can ruin hopes for a championship or a world title for the year.

Many riders have made it to their breed world or national shows for the first time using the techniques learned from my "Resistance-Free Riding" video. These techniques have also made a major difference for those who never wish to compete with their horses, but simply to enjoy them out on the trail and at home as companions and friends.

In my life with horses, I have witnessed all levels of riders and horses in the show ring, triumphing in winning, or exiting in defeat. I have been a part of those moments for many people as their trainer, instructor, or judge. All my life I've been looking for what makes the perfect horse, the perfect ride, the perfect rider. It seemed as though it had to be something magic because only a chosen few had this quality and ability. I analyzed the qualities shared by top riders and used this information in developing the ideas behind resistance-free riding.

I was raised on an Oregon horse ranch. There was always a lot of stock to ride and horses around for sale. I often showed horses to buyers. I learned very early that you couldn't fight with a horse if you wanted it to look its best and bring top dollar.

When I was riding young horses, I watched many of the other riders. Some of the old-timers were absolutely part of the horse. Other riders were always at war with their horses, and it showed in their riding.

As a boy, I thought that the gift to make a new horse give his ultimate for you in the stress of training was gypsy magic. When I moved from the ranch into the show ring, I noticed that some of the other riders had that magical quality. There would always be one standout who could win the class with little effort. Such riders were always called the "natural" riders. The same held true for the professional trainers. Some of them sweated bullets and got little result; others simply sailed through the class and picked up their blue ribbons on the way out.

When I was showing, I did not always have the fanciest horse in the class, but I learned how to take an average horse, get the best out of him, and ride out with a good ribbon, or even the silver. I was lucky to do some good winning at a level that was really beyond the reach of those horses.

I learned, as I went along, from some of the greatest riders and trainers of the time, in all disciplines. I had the advantage of being a member of a local saddle club located at the state fairgrounds. Almost every month a different horseman was in the area teaching and training. It might be a cutting-horse man one week or a jumper trainer the next. I honed my skills until I achieved success at the top, fortunately winning over those who had been my ideals.

At that time most of the major shows were mixed shows with many disciplines, such as Western, gaited, hunter-jumper, and driving. There could be a jumper or a reiner tuning up in the center of the ring while someone else warmed up a five-gaited horse on the rail. Mixed-breed shows are becoming less common, and it is a sad thing. We can all learn from one another as I have.

When I opened a training barn, I knew I couldn't be satisfied with just showing in the Northwest. I joined with some other professional horsemen to form a professional horsemen's organization that sponsored seminars and clinics, bringing the level of Northwest riding on par with other parts of the United States. The competition between all of us young professionals helped improve our skills. Other Northwest professionals and instructors started taking their horses and students to national shows, and I thought, "Why can't I start showing back east?" My sights were raised to national levels instead of just the big shows on the West Coast. A trainer had to have the students and horses to compete on a national level, or he or she didn't stay there. It was a challenge to prove that I and my students belonged there with all the rest.

Learning about the West Coast bridle horse was very important in my development. I was impressed with the perfection of a horse who could switch leads every other stride and slide forty feet. I realized that it took more than just a nice horse. In my early twenties, I began winning at major shows, beating many other top riders. After that breakthrough, I found it easy to go back east and compete.

There I saw riders using split reins and other techniques. I found that to compete with those people I had to get fine-tuned to their level of skill. In turn they began to accept me, and I participated in many national-level activities, which included the making of a film for the American Quarter Horse Association (AQHA).

I was soon asked to give my first lecture and demonstration at the All-American Quarter Horse Congress, in Columbus, Ohio, which was a significant honor, as it is the largest horse event in the world. Since that time I've given more than a dozen demonstrations and lectures at the Congress. My demonstration riders and I got a standing ovation from the Congress audience. For the first time through visualizations I call "word pictures" and a program of watching the rider right in harmony with the horse, the general public began to see that they could learn "feel." They could refine their abilities to really know and improve their horse and them-selves without limits.

I got to see the top hands and compete with the best stock, seeing that little edge that could either make or break you. No matter how good your horse, if you didn't have the riding skills, it didn't happen for you in the ring.

I judged my first show—at a small show in Oregon—as a

teenager. I found judging challenging because it was a total commitment to understanding, knowing, and looking for the real finish, rather than just going into the ring and saying I competed. That led to judging on judging teams, which included giving oral explanations for my selections and competing as a judge. I was lucky enough to also get to judge a lot of schooling shows and playdays.

I became an American Horse Shows Association (AHSA) judge at twenty-one, junior judging under many top officials from both east and west, which was a great education. I have since been invited to judge more than a thousand shows, including eleven world championships for four different breeds. I have judged the AHSA Stock Seat Medal Finals three times and the International Stock Seat Medal Finals twice. I have also been licensed as a judge by the American Quarter Horse Association, the American Paint Horse Association, the Appaloosa Horse Club, and the International Arabian Horse Association.

I was also a member of the AHSA Stock Seat Committee for a number of years, which gave me a chance to contribute to the sport at a national level. It also let me confer and focus on riding with other top judges and exhibitors.

Whenever I was on a judging assignment, I spent a lot of time talking to my fellow judges during breaks and in the evenings. I discovered that we were all looking for that same quality that separated the champion from the rest. It can be very challenging to select a top horse when every horse in the arena is a multiple champion. It was always assumed that the ability to create magic under saddle was one that was God-given, not learned.

I saw some fine rides while working as a judge, sharing and learning from my colleagues at the same time. I learned from them about their specialties and judged side by side with them through some very long days. As a judge I started to perfect my eye for that genuine feel and finish on a rider. It was the icing on the cake. Judging at the world show level for different breeds also taught me a lot about harmony and that great ride that makes the hair on your arms stand up. It gave me a base from which I started to mold my ideas.

I started youth clinics at our barn and progressed to doing week-long clinics worldwide. I'm proud to have helped develop youth and world champions, and I was the first instructor to have a student from another nation win at the Quarter Horse Youth

World Championships. Many riders came through my clinics and I was the better for it. It was a tremendous challenge. Many of these students were successful at a national level.

I was also the coach of the U.S. team that went to Australia for World Cup competition competing in AQHA classes. I found that this situation offered a different sort of challenge, as I only met these team members a week before the competition, and there literally was not time to "take them apart and put them back together." I used resistance-free riding techniques to make slight changes in their positions that would improve their ability, but not such radical changes that the rider would lose self-confidence.

In a situation like this, where you can't go back and redo the basics, you make do with what you have and fix the little things. I didn't strive for ultimate perfection from each rider, but went for overall improvement, fixing the most important things to a satisfactory level. This way I got more from these riders than I would have any other way.

Experiences like this one, and at many clinics worldwide, showed me how to make the most of short-term teaching situations and send riders home with a better set of skills. In addition, I saw that a horse trainer is no better than his or her horse, and the horse is no better than its rider. I worked with both gifted horses and riders, which made the training easy, and I became very aware of their natural skills. I wanted to try and share some of that natural ability with the less gifted people. I wanted to be able to inspire not only the superstar, but the rider who didn't have the feel.

If I hadn't ridden lots of young horses as a youngster, followed by gaining lots of mileage on the show circuit as a competitor, trainer and judge, I wouldn't have had the background to help these people. I found that through these clinics I had many opportunities to learn by trial and error the best way to put information across.

I am still learning. I read articles on other sports and figure out ways they relate to riding. A ski lesson with my son can give me fresh input on how to teach something to my own students.

I have done many, many horsemanship clinics over the years as well and learned that nothing is more important than communication. As I learned how to better express myself, I began to develop the principles that became resistance-free riding. I've done clinics all around the world and learned how to convey ideas to people who spoke little or no English. Some of them didn't even have saddles.

Through my students, I have shared in many wonderful moments as they achieved complete harmony with their horses, resulting in many successes—including World Championship placements. I owe a great deal to these students, as they taught me while I was teaching them. I also have a boundless debt to the many great horsemen and horsewomen who took the time to share some of their knowledge with me along the way.

When I began teaching, I noticed that about 5 percent of my students had that "natural" magic. They were the ones that made me famous as an instructor because they would be winning all the time. I began to look for these potential champions. They would always come through on a consistent basis and end up as a world champion later down the line.

I began to experiment with ways to help the remaining 95 percent improve their riding. I discovered various drills and exercises that made it possible for these riders to learn the feel that the top 5 percent had innately. I learned visualization techniques that helped my students understand what I wanted to say, no matter what their language. The traditional instructors swore I could not teach the magic of feel, but I began to see it happen, again and again.

Our office has gotten many letters from riders who have seen a major change in their abilities, often achieving success beyond their wildest dreams. Cutters and reiners have added two or three points to their scores, the significant two or three points that often make the difference between first and second. Ropers, barrel racers, and other speed-event riders find that their times have improved, sometimes by several seconds, placing them higher in the standings. Pleasure horse riders have developed the ability to keep a marching rhythm that resulted in top ribbons. Endurance riders have noticed that they were far more comfortable during long hours in the saddle, and that their horses performed beyond their expectations because they were no longer interfering with the horses' movement.

Even riders who no longer compete can enjoy the benefits of resistance-free riding. They no longer ache after a day of trail riding.

The riders that worked for every improvement and developed their talents to the fullest became the masters, like the Swiss watchmaker working with 250 tiny parts. They learned to know each part, which then gave them the special skill to make refined adjustments in the final product.

Natural riders often seemed to lack some of the ability to do the fine tuning because they had never had to work at it like the other riders. They settled for what came naturally and took it no further.

If you aren't a natural rider, take heart. You know what you want and you can have it.

Today you have a choice. You can learn and improve to a new level. How far you take that improvement is strictly up to you. You can stop wishing you were born with "feel."

The rider armed with the skills of resistance-free riding will always win the battle.

❀ ❀ ❀

PART ONE

❀ ❀ ❀

Part One introduces you to the concepts of resistance-free horsemanship, showing how to develop the unity with the horse and the refinement of the aids necessary to achieve both success in competition and satisfaction at home.

1

❀ ❀ ❀

Relaxation Equals Confidence

An average rider can become a good rider, and a good rider can become a top hand through resistance-free techniques. Excellent riders with motivation can go even further—to compete at national levels and beyond. Time and time again at clinics I see people make radical changes in their ability over the course of a weekend just by gaining confidence.

I believe the key to success is confidence, no matter what the sport or activity. If you show riders of ordinary talent how to become confident through relaxation, they can ride beyond their wildest dreams. Riders with ordinary horses can outperform better-mounted competitors.

Observe the competitors in any sport. The one thing that a world champion does is maximize his or her talent and ability at their peak. The common thread in any sport is that the champions can make it look so easy. The incredible leaps of an Olympic ice

Confidence is an unmistakable quality in the performance of horse and rider.

skater become possible through relaxation and confidence. We have all seen what happens when a skater becomes rattled after a fall, or gets "psyched out" by the importance of the competition, or just can't get it together. A true champion can recover from a setback and go on to finish with a flourish.

Relaxation and confidence make it possible for top-class high divers to glide into the pool with the smallest of splashes. A moment of lost concentration or shakiness can result in a belly flop that is painful both physically and emotionally. Yet, when all goes well, it looks easy.

Professional athletes bat home runs, snag passes, and dunk baskets with ease when they are at the top of their game. The same is seen in the horse world, whatever the event. Slides and lead changes become fluid and effortless. Hunters and jumpers float over their fences. Gymkhana horses sail through their courses without an instant of wasted effort.

Unfortunately we've all seen what happens when horse and rider get tense and lose their confidence. Just as in other sports, a moment of hesitation can result in a mistake, an awkward moment, or even a fall.

A tight, nervous rider is his or her own worst enemy. Nerves can undo weeks and months of practice. Your first and most important concern is not to defeat yourself before you begin. Your competitors will never need to give you a second look as long as you trash your own rides.

I see Western-pleasure riders getting nervous and overcueing the horse, causing unbalanced, stiff transitions. A reiner might get nervous and jerk the horse without preparing him for a good stop, resulting in a bouncy stop on the forehand and probably a sky-high head as well. A barrel racer can override the course and waste precious time rounding the barrels after coming in with too much uncontrolled speed.

A cutting-horse rider who freezes can literally take the "cow" right out of his horse. The horse stops paying attention to the cow and focuses instead on the rider, who suddenly isn't a whole lot of help up there.

Tension problems are especially common with riders who show over fences, even in hunter hack with the smallest of obstacles. That tension can be transmitted to the horse, who might rocket wildly from fence to fence, making the rider still more anxious. Or you might see the rider creeping around the course, stifling the horse's movement and causing the horse to chip at the fences, all because of the rider's nervousness.

One of the most precision-oriented events is western trail class; a good trail rider can maneuver through a course as though he or she were a centaur. Tension breaks the lines of communication, causing the horse to step off the bridge, tick the walk-overs, or otherwise lose its concentration.

It Starts with the Rider

As you can see, many common problems have their roots in a tense rider. I break these patterns down into red-light and green-light situations.

A cutting horse can only do its job well if the rider is not interfering.

The green light goes on for a relaxed, confident rider who shows total harmony and unity with his or her horse; the two are mentally and physically attuned as one. Their transitions are fluid and nonresistant, occurring almost with the rider's thoughts and invisible aids. The horse performs to its utmost ability, and the rider makes it look easy.

The red-light performance shows a lot of anticipation on the part of the horse and rider. In response to the rider's nervousness, the horse stiffens, loses its frame, and becomes inconsistent in its gait. Its rhythm begins to break up. The red-light rider shows no consistency through his or her pattern. The horse might be lazy and inattentive, or hyperactive and over-responsive. The two simply haven't got it together.

By nature, the horse is a herd animal who thrives on being dominated. In the wild, the herd will be led by a dominant mare who makes most of the decisions. The stallion has other things on his mind. The rest of the herd members go along with whatever the lead mare decides.

In domestic life, you have to be your horse's "leader" in order to be successful. When you have gained your horse's trust and respect, you can ask the horse to literally jump through fire. . . and the horse will do it.

Different horse sports have different requirements. Everyone knows about the faithful school horse who can do a hunter course carrying a potato sack and win the class. Once the horse knows its job, it can perform on autopilot as long as you, the rider, do not interfere by giving clashing aids or otherwise making it impossible for the horse to work.

Five Master Keys Can Change Your Riding Forever

Resistance-free horsemanship consists of five keys that will enable you to unlock the door to becoming a master rider. These five keys are:

OPEN EYES
BREATHING
PREPARATORY COMMANDS
THE RIPPLE EFFECT
POSITIVE MENTAL PREPARATION

You use your eyes for an awareness that creates the necessary relaxation to make things work. Proper breathing preserves that relaxation for both horse and rider. Correct rider position enables the horse to position himself correctly as well. Without correct position, you handicap yourself and lose the confidence of the horse.

Preparatory commands let the rider assume the role of leader, giving the horse the security and the assuredness required to make it brave, alert, and responsive. The ripple effect, explained in Chapter 9, gives you the feel of energy from the horse's footfalls.

All of these points require one more tool to make them work: a positive mental attitude. Without that, you haven't got the winning ingredient.

We've looked at the importance of confidence in the process of becoming a master rider. In the next chapters, we'll look at how these other keys fit into your program of improvement. We'll also explore the importance of position, hands, and balance.

Confidence is the master key to success in resistance-free riding as well as in life.

2

❀ ❀ ❀

Position of the Foot and Leg

The position and organization of the rider's lower body creates a solid foundation for the resistance-free rider. The correct position of the foot and leg are essential for a rider to be effective.

The Foot

Foot position is very important in the complete rider. Whatever you do with your leg affects your shoulders, and your foot position reflects what occurs above.

The resistance-free rider definitely rides off of the ball of his or her foot. The foot is not shoved "home" all the way into the stirrup. When the stirrup is at the ball of the foot, it allows the ankle to act as a shock absorber.

If the resistance-free rider places more weight on the inside of

Total harmony between horse and rider creates optimum performance.

the foot up toward the big toe, he or she makes a tremendous gain in equilibrium. This is reflected in research into the best type of shoe for runners and walkers. Motion studies show that the big toe is extremely important in balance and equilibrium.

For the rider, the big toe acts almost as an indicator. If the foot is "all the way home," this indicator is not very useful, as everything is locked into place. Placing weight toward the inside and toward the big toe gives much more flexibility.

Many cutters and timed-event riders ride "home" due to the influence of the old-time cowboys, who believed that you were more stable if your feet were placed all the way home in the stirrups. If it worked for the bronc rider, it had to work for the barrel racer, or so they thought.

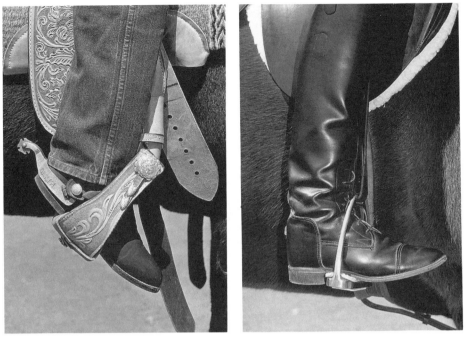

The foot position in these photographs creates resistance in the horse as well as contributing to a rigid, stiff-bodied rider who cannot follow the horse's movement. Rather than creating security, this foot position creates stiffness.

The rider who places only the toe in the stirrup sacrifices security and limits the use of the leg.

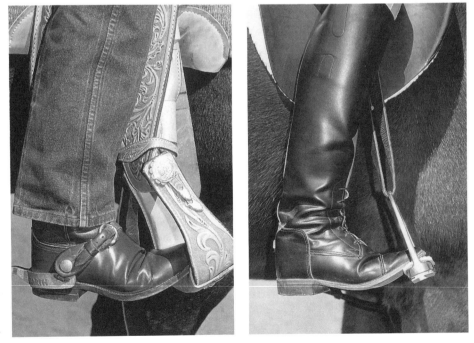

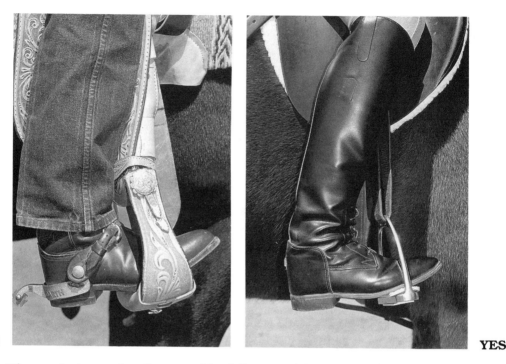

YES   **YES**

These photographs show an ideal foot position that allows the rider maximum flexibility and responsiveness to the movements of the horse.

Many of my cutting-horse friends say, "I'm already posting a seventy-three or a seventy-four score with my foot all the way home. Why should I change?"

I tell them, "With that extra flexibility in the foot and ankle, you might be posting seventy-five or seventy-six."

In contrast, the resistance-free rider needs to have more freedom in his or her foot to be able to pick up that first vibration that warns of an approaching movement or action. Just as a radio is fine-tuned to pick up a station, the rider is tuned acutely into what the horse is broadcasting.

The ankle is an important shock absorber, and the joints of the foot are secondary shock absorbers. If any part of the foot or ankle is jammed into position, the shock absorber effect is lost, and with it, a critical part of your ability to be in harmony with your horse.

People who are naturally splayfooted (toe-out) will find it harder to get their legs and feet into good position. They will be inclined to point their toes outward, and they will contact the horse's ribs mostly with the back of their leg. They will also have less flexibility because the joints are rotating outward.

A sure indicator of whether you are maintaining good leg and foot position while riding is to notice where your riding boots or chaps are getting dirty. If there is dirt along the back seam and a big sweat stain, you're toeing out big time. The ideal is to get the *inside* of the calf dirty, not the back of the calf.

If you are a splayfooted person, correcting the problem on a long-term basis will call for work on the ground as well as on the horse. One Olympic dressage rider was plagued with just such a problem and finally resolved to cure it one winter. She walked pigeon-toed all winter long and was very uncomfortable, but by spring, she was straight.

If your toes point out excessively, you will have a greater tendency to use the spur first, instead of the calf, to cue the horse. You will also be bumping fence posts, trail obstacles, and other horses when you get too close. Trying to ride on both sides of a

Riders with this toe-out leg position are not able to use their lower legs to best effect in cuing the horse, nor are they able to follow the horse easily in fast maneuvers.

NO   **NO**

fence post at the same time may give you a very good reason to correct the problem.

The Lower Leg

When the lower leg is correctly angled and positioned, it works as a place of security, a guide, and an energy and rhythm collector, as well as a confidence builder.

The lower leg should always be secure and steady. The rider who lacks lower leg organization will have horses respond in an insecure manner. As the leg floats around giving the signals to the horse's side in a different spot each time. It's a guaranteed way to lose refined communication. It's like typing on a computer with your fingers one row off. Your lower leg should be as secure and firm as your hand is when leading a young child through traffic on a busy highway. With both the upper and lower leg, the angle must be correct in order to be effective. This angle varies, depending on the sport; however, the angle between the thigh and the lower leg and the angle between the ankle and the foot must be the same.

This position takes the lower leg completely away from the horse, making it difficult to use the leg subtly and correctly.

NO   NO

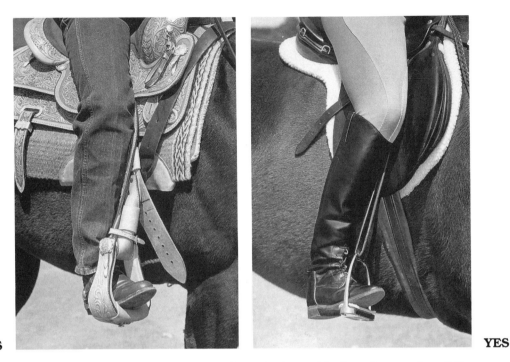

YES   YES

The lower leg gives you a good foundation. Notice the angle of the lower leg and thigh.

If the rider braces the lower leg forward, the angle of the lower leg in relation to the thigh changes, and is no longer the same as the angle of the thigh to the pelvis. In correct position, these angles are identical.

The Upper Leg and Knee

The upper leg has some of the largest muscle groups found in the body. It plays a major role in giving strength to the rider's position.

Your leg position is closely connected to your seat position. It is nearly impossible to change the position of the upper leg without affecting the position of the seat. When one changes, so does the other.

The knee is the connection between the upper and lower legs, offering a point of shock absorption that is very important. It is the means by which a rider can soften the ride, absorbing the jarring (if any) given by the horse. The knee, coupled with the ankle, lets

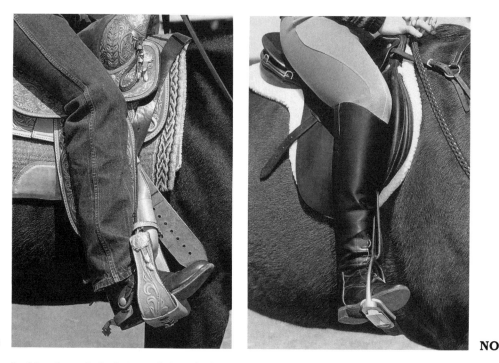

NO   **NO**

A rider in a "chair" position is bracing behind the motion of the horse and is not able to ride effectively.

you soak up motion and remain glued to the horse instead of bouncing off the saddle. As a rider, you will become increasingly softer as your knee's ability to absorb movement improves.

The hinge of the knee determines the angulation of the upper and lower leg. If the knee gets too far forward, the rider ends up sitting behind the horse in a chair position. If the knee is too far back, the rider loses stability in the upper body and tends to get ahead of the horse.

In the old days riders were encouraged to grip hard or pinch with their knees. It really sounded good when we told our students to act as if they had a bolt going from one knee to the other, right through the horse. That did work for the rail rider. However, when the rider needed to use his or her seat in order to drive the horse forward, the impulsion wasn't there. The harder the rider squeezed his or her knees, the further the seat came out of the saddle, and the more unstable the rider became. The rider lost connection with the horse, especially in transitions up and down.

Now trainers like to see a soft knee, well lowered, that lets the rider sit down close to the horse, literally wrapping over the horse's body like hot candle wax dripping over the candlestick.

Novice riders often dismount after a short ride and have difficulty walking. That is because they are not only gripping with their knees, but with their thighs as well, counting on muscle power rather than balance to keep them on the horse. This makes the legs very sore, and the added stress of continually maintaining this clamping results in a rider who is tense throughout the body. As noted earlier, tension and confidence don't associate with one another. A rider without confidence cannot relax, cannot trust the horse. The horse isn't having a good time, either, because it is busy packing around the Human Clamp.

The Human Clamp responds to every transition and movement by achieving the impossible: applying more leg pressure. No wonder he or she dismounts and can't walk.

Since the upper and lower leg work in close concert with the rider's seat, riders who have increased their ability to use the upper leg will enjoy an advantage over other riders. The upper leg plays an important role in stabilizing the seat of riders during performances. The reiner will discover that his or her seat has extra power and drive to use in those long hard stops. Cow penners will stay in balance when they make those hard wall turns, driving to the cow's head in order to make a save. Instead of lurching over the horse's shoulder, well-seated riders remain centered on the horse as it abruptly changes direction.

Even team ropers make their runs standing in their stirrups, counting on the stability given by their upper leg contact to give them a steady platform for making a throw. After all, how many competitive ropers have you seen that made their runs sitting on their pockets? I hope it isn't many. We know those riders won't make it to the National Finals Rodeo in Las Vegas.

Adjusting Stirrup Length

Finding the correct adjustment of the stirrups is essential to being able to use your upper leg to your best advantage. The shorter the stirrup, the more extreme the angles of the leg, and the more powerful and stable your position becomes. It is crucial that the knee remains lowered and the foot stays back beneath the knee: it is easy for the rider with poor basics to thrust his or her lower legs forward to try to find more security.

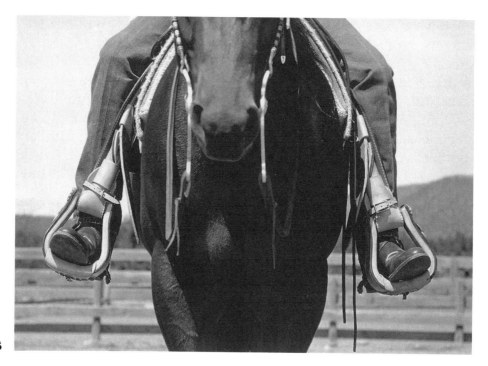

YES

It is of the utmost importance that the stirrups be even for good balance.

YES

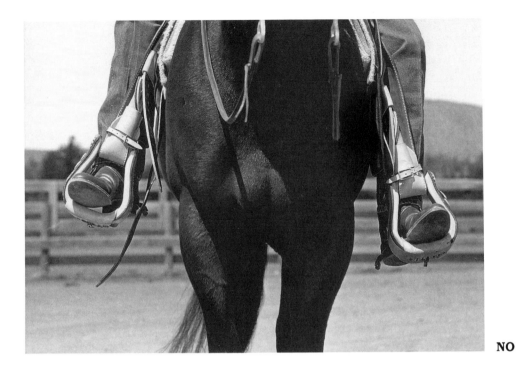

NO

One longer stirrup can distort the position of your upper body and result in a loss of balance.

NO

You see most cutters and cow penners riding in fairly short stirrups because of the speed and fast turns in their sports. Reiners, who do a lot of lateral work in circles, tend to ride with a little longer stirrup.

It is also important that your stirrups are even. Because you mount from the left, the left stirrup tends to stretch over time, causing your body to shift off center in order to retain a feel of the left stirrup. This throws the horse off balance and will seriously inhibit your work to the right.

Leg Pressure and Control

The rider who has control of the horse's hindquarters is a rider who is in control of the horse. As soon as you can use your legs to

You'll find shorter stirrups used for timed events such as cattle penning.

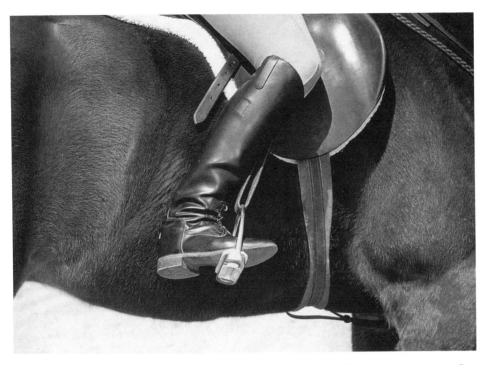

On a horse who is insensitive to the leg, you may have to use your leg further back when giving cues.

ask your horse to move away from pressure, you are able to hold the horse in position with your legs.

It is important to determine the right amount of pressure to apply to each horse you ride. Some horses are responsive to pressure as subtle as the slightest tightening of the calf muscle, as light as a breath of air. Other horses require several pounds of pressure, often with the backup aid of the spur. Some horses who are dull-sided need to have the lower leg used back toward the flank or lower on the belly, where they are a little more sensitive.

The resistance-free rider always uses the right amount of pressure. The right amount of pressure is defined as the exact amount—and no more—that it takes to get the desired response. The quickest way to have a colt stampede is to scare it with excess leg pressure before it's ready. You can also ruin a sensitive horse by using excessive pressure and teaching it to tune out your cues.

Riders who tend to pound or kick instead of squeeze will create horses who respond only to these crude aids. I like to use the expression, "Less is more." You can school a horse to respond to a subtle aid very easily. Not only does this improve the horse's

You can educate yourself and your horse to coordinate smoothly together without resistance with the use of simple exercises like the turn on the forehand. At the beginning level, the horse should be bent away from the direction of movement and make tiny steps forward around the stationary leg. The horse is bent in an arc around the rider's leg.

performance, but it enables you as the rider to communicate with only minimal muscle movements that are almost invisible to the observer.

Would you rather be slugged in the ribs or tapped when someone wants to get your attention?

I hope you'd rather be tapped.

Remember that a whisper is as good as a shout if the horse is listening. A horse can feel a fly on its hip, so it obviously notices your every movement. It's up to you to make those movements mean something.

Educate the horse as to the meaning of the leg by urging the horse forward lightly with your leg. Many times the leg aid is more effective if used with a slight forward motion, against the grain of the horse's hair, rather than a backward kick that tends to disconnect the horse's hindquarters. A forward motion that ruffles the hair makes a lighter movement even more noticeable by the horse.

I like to think of my legs as a whisk broom, making little short movements instead of one big long stroke, driving the horse forward. I tell my students that one long stroke leaves the dirt behind, whereas little sweeps pick up the dirt and do the job.

Often, if the horse has not been schooled properly, the first light cue gets no response. Ask again, this time reinforcing the cue with the spur or the whip as well as a slightly firmer leg aid. Repeat, increasing the intensity of the cues, until you get a response. If the horse takes off at a trot or canter, and you were just asking for a walk, don't punish it. Instead, come back to the walk softly and let the horse understand that forward was the right response. The only wrong thing was the amount of forward movement it gave.

Next, repeat the original light aid. If the horse responds, you've achieved your goal. If not, repeat the previous sequence. The horse must learn that everything is easier if it responds to that first light cue; otherwise you're going to make it more uncomfortable.

The key is to teach the horse that the light aid is the desirable one. Don't let the horse trap you into always asking for a lope with a clunk of the leg, just because the horse tunes out everything else. You can reprogram the horse if you are consistent in always returning to exactly the same light aid as the first step in making a movement or transition.

Once your leg pressure is tuned in to the appropriate level of feel for your horse, it's easy to guide and place the horse's body as you wish. I refer to the body because the resistance-free rider can control the horse's hip, rib cage, back, and shoulder, gaining rider control of leads, circles, lead changes, and stops, as well as cadence and collection. (Elementary exercises such as the turn on the forehand, the turn on the haunches, the side-pass and two-tracking help establish your communication system with the horse.)

When you ask your horse for either lead, all you need to do is use an outside leg to move the horse's hip in the direction of the lead you want. Leads on your horse will never become a problem. With practice, you will not need to actually move the hip over. Just the "feel" of positioning them will be sufficient to tell your horse what you desire. More sophisticated forms of riding will add the influence of the inside leg to create refinement and straightness in the strike-off.

The horse should remain as straight as possible and maintain its frame. This is achieved by using your legs like a whisk broom with the rhythm of the footfalls to gather the horse into light

Your horse will always do what you ask if you position its body correctly beforehand. This horse is being prepared for a strike-off on the left lead.

YES

This is a common sight with novice riders as they try to chase the horse into the lope instead of giving preparatory commands that alert and position the horse to lope.

NO

collection. Crude aids for asking the horse to lope, such as turning the horse's head into the fence before pulling the horse back around and kicking with the outside leg, have no place in resistance-free horsemanship. That's like shouting at someone who doesn't understand English, on the theory that he just might grasp the words if you make them loud enough. The unschooled horse is just as confused as the foreign visitor. Neither of them have the slightest idea what you are shouting about.

When you learn to use subtle leg aids, circles and turns become easy because you can adjust the degree of bend to the exact amount required. The horse wraps around your inside leg in a smooth arc that resembles a rainbow or a banana. The outside leg holds the hip and rib cage in the arc, preventing the horse from drifting outward and evading the aids. The outside leg becomes a wall, but a very smart wall—one that can open, one that can shape, one that can guide. If you can push something, you can also hold it.

Lead changes become easy, as you'll discover later in the section on reining. With proper leg control (controlling the horse's rib cage and hip with your leg), the horse can be positioned to change behind first. This is the correct way to change leads, and it also ensures that the horse will not drop a hind lead. You will learn how the release of the leg during a change will help your horse through a quiet, correct change.

When the resistance-free rider learns to develop cadence and rhythm with horses, he or she soon realizes that the leg works a lot like a drumstick is used by a drummer. The rider must learn to use the lower leg in time and rhythm with the horse's footfalls before he or she can be in true harmony with the horse. This timing allows the rider to become part of the inner horse, part of the horse's movement. They are no longer a horse and a rider, but a unit that works and thinks as one. Feel develops between horse and rider, and the rider learns how much aid it takes to communicate with each individual horse. The amount of lower leg aid will vary according to whether the horse is numb-sided, or of a quiet disposition, or the level of training present.

Resistance-free riders learn that the stronger the leg aid, the stronger the cadence. The lighter the leg aid, the weaker the cadence. By stronger, I don't mean upgrading the leg aid to a kick or to squeeze the horse in two. I'm referring to a more positive contact that is meaningful to the horse, as opposed to a wispy,

You can clearly see a correct bend in these horses' bodies as they shape themselves to the circle in obedience to the riders' aids.

inconsistent touch that may not register with the horse. Since the rider's seat and legs are the foundation of resistance-free riding, it is important for the resistance-free rider to develop this important link in the chain.

Good Horses Teach Good Riders

One of the real tragedies I encounter at my seminars are the riders who have learned to ride on horses who didn't have a clue about leg aids. It's like trying to teach someone to drive a car by using a car that doesn't have any brakes, accelerator, or steering.

The greatest gift you can give a rider who is just learning is to let him or her start on the best trained horse you can find. I was fortunate enough to start my son, Justin, on an old reiner that I had in the barn. He never learned to pull or kick hard. That sensitivity will last him for the rest of his life.

Every time I watch a proud parent try to teach his or her child how to ride on an untrained pony who doesn't have the slightest

A well-trained pony will be a special friend for everyone it meets. Ponies are highly suitable for small riders because the animals' size makes them less intimidating and easier to ride correctly.

Young riders learn more than just horsemanship when they have a horse. They learn determination, patience, and judgment.

desire to cooperate, I hold my breath. The youngster's first priority is always to survive. In order to do this, he or she may yank the reins to make sure that the animal will stop, or turn, or the child may flap both legs clear off the horse in an effort to flail the beast into motion. It usually ends in a contest to find out who is the toughest—and the pony usually wins. I am not saying that all ponies are numb-sided or hardmouthed, because there are a lot of well-trained ponies out there. An educated pony is worth its weight in gold. I have judged the Pony of Americas World and National Championship shows and have the greatest respect for them. They can perform as well as their larger colleagues. Of course, training is the key.

So often ignorant people assume that because they are small, ponies don't need training. Some ponies are too small to be ridden by adults, and therefore learn bad manners. If you have such a pony, find a talented teenager and have him or her teach the pony so that it can teach the child.

Exercises to Improve the Use of Your Feet and Legs

Here are a number of good drills for improving your use of your feet:

1. Try standing and sitting in the saddle, 5 strides standing and 5 strides sitting.
2. Drop and pick up stirrups without looking, repeating frequently.
3. Practice changing gaits, concentrating on flexibility in the ankle.
4. Rotate your toe out and in as you trot along. Your weight should fall to the inside of your foot, not the outside. The more variation you can get in your foot position, the easier it will be for your feet to settle into a position that is correct and effective.

The following exercises will help you develop your ability to use your legs:

1. Stand about one step away from a wall and place your hands against the wall at shoulder height. Stand in a

buttress position with one leg ahead of the other. The foot on the leg that is extended back should be pressed flat, first pressing down on the toes and then extending the heel to the ground.

You can feel how this lengthens your hamstring and increases the amount of stretch available. Do this exercise slowly, as this helps prevent tearing injuries and also increases the training effect.

Switch leg positions and exercise the other leg. Repeat this a number of times.

2. Stand on the edge of a step or rail, balanced on your toes, and extend both heels down over the edge. You'll need to hold onto a railing for balance.

3. Sit in a chair, holding a fairly large beach ball between your legs (a thigh exerciser would also work). Squeeze with both knees and release. Repeat this twenty-five times. Your knees benefit from this exercise.

4. Trot over cavalletti at appropriate spacing while standing in the stirrups, letting your knees absorb the shock. For the Western jog, allow about three feet between each pole. For English riders the distance varies; allow from four and a half or more, depending on the horse's length of stride.

5. For the upper leg, I like to see riders work at the lope or canter. Drop both stirrups and rise up off of the saddle for ten strides, then sit ten. Begin by repeating this exercise twice, and work gradually until you can repeat the sequence eight times.

Great resistance-free riders are perfected, not by strength, but by a solid foundation.

CASE STUDY 9071: *Ruth is thirty years old, single, and spends a lot of time with her horse. She started out riding saddle seat and has since switched to stock seat. The horse she rides needs spurs to get a good response. The trouble is that the horse sticks in his transitions and doesn't react promptly, and when he does respond, he overreacts, almost jumping out of his skin and abruptly changing*

Good riding begins with work on the ground. The buttress exercise helps lengthen your hamstrings and increase the amount of stretch you can achieve.

Steps or rails can be useful for improving your ability to get your heels down, increasing your overall flexibility.

gait or direction. This puts her out of the ribbons because the horse just isn't fitting the picture of a pliable, soft ride.

A video tape reveals that she's not jabbing the horse with the spurs, so what is happening?

The first clue to Ruth's problem is that she said she used to ride saddle seat.

Many old-style saddle-seat riders learn to hold their legs in a stiff position, the leg below the knee not touching the horse. They are balancing completely on their seat while maintaining a chair pose. You used to see this a lot in photos; the pose looks completely artificial.

These same people would ride Western in the same manner, holding their legs away from the horse. This was the style for a few years until it was realized that this pose (and that's all it was) wasn't really good horsemanship. When you asked these "posers" to turn back a cow or "ride 'em and slide 'em," they couldn't stay on the horse as well. Some of them hit the dirt with their legs still in that same rigid pose!

Ruth is riding with a rigid, forced lower leg that places the heel and spur far from the horse's side. In order for her to use the spurs, she has to make a much greater movement with her leg than necessary and often ends up overcueing and bruising the horse instead of giving a light touch.

If she softens and turns her toe out slightly, the heel and spur will be closer to the horse. This should not be exaggerated, or the spurs will be in the horse all of the time, and that is not the idea. She must learn how to use her heel and lower leg instead of just poking with the spur for a cue. The spur is a reinforcement, not the means of giving the order.

If the horse learns to respond to light aids, such as the touch of the calf, he will continue to respect the spur, which is held in reserve for those times when he fails to respond promptly or completely to an aid.

This rider must give her horse a preparatory command before

(facing page)
Work without stirrups is one of the ultimate ways to improve your riding and make you one with your horse. By alternating standing and sitting without stirrups, you avoid excessive strain while improving your ability to move from position to position.

turning her heel up and sticking the horse with the spur. If the horse is not prepared for a command, he will respond abruptly, in an out-of-balance manner, or worse, not at all, or very slowly.

The lower leg is really the tool that enables you to ride "into the horse," giving you a means to ask the horse to use its back. You should have a 45-degree angle in the upper leg as well as the lower leg, with both angles matching.

Most Western riders have too closed an angle between their thigh and body, placing them in a chair seat. If you're in that chair position with the lower leg vertical, you automatically place the horse on its forehand and give it a sore back.

Ten years ago we taught riders to clamp with the knee and this forced the lower legs away from the horse. It also forced the seat up off of the back. Keep in mind that you want to feel as though you were riding in a Cadillac with soft springs rather than a four-wheel-drive truck, taking shock and not reflecting any of it into the horse.

A good exercise is to trot around the arena for two or three minutes, posting five strides, sitting five, posting ten, sitting ten,

This exercise looks strange, but it really teaches you how to get your weight into your heels.

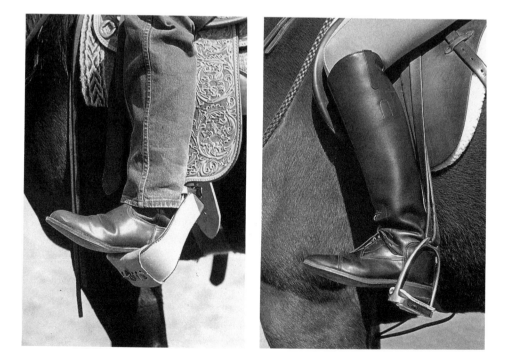

and repeating this sequence again and again. To add more difficulty, do this exercise with your arms held out to the sides like an airplane. (This exercise is best done in a round pen or a small arena unless the horses are very quiet.)

Another good exercise to help riders who can't get enough weight into their heels is to have them practice with their heels in the stirrup from the front. This can be done either English or Western. It appears strange, but it's very effective.

Challenges can be stepping stones or stumbling blocks. It's how you use them that counts.

3

❀ ❀ ❀

Position of the Back and Upper Body

The upper body position and organization help create correct posture and an overall balanced look for the resistance-free rider.

The middle of the back is like the clutch on a car. It absorbs energy and connects the upper body to the horse.

We used to see riders with stiff backs, rigid as pokers. Their lines were good, and that's what we thought mattered at the time. Now we ask for a rider to breathe with the upper third of his or her body, and this gives the rider an elegant upper posture, or as I like to think of it, the look of an eagle. This keeps the upper body up off the hips.

It used to seem as though the short-waisted rider had an edge because he or she was closer to the ground, so to speak, and was more stable with a lower center of gravity. I'm now looking for an athletic, balanced rider, because there needs to be a softness in the back. While extremes sometimes seem to be an advantage, over the long haul they aren't such an advantage after all.

The soft back is the equalizer that makes riding look easy; you always see one in the natural rider. A soft back can develop cadence and rhythm for the rail horse, and make the rough pleasure horse look smooth. A soft back keeps good flat changes in your reiners and Western riding horses. Soft backs make long slides.

When I see a soft back on a cutter, I see a rider who is really down and soft into the horse. For the hunter-jumper rider, a soft back makes two-point work much more comfortable, effective, and balanced. Rigidity can result in a sore back for the rider. Barrel racers will find that a soft back absorbs the energy as the horse rounds the barrels.

Men and Women Ride Differently

Everyone who has ever noticed that there is a difference between men and women, raise your hand.

I find that the upper body is very important to the stability and effectiveness of the seat. The way you use your shoulders and upper body influences how the rest of your body reacts.

Here's where men and women are very different. Men tend to have more problems with their upper bodies because they usually are broader and more muscular than a woman's. This brings a man's center of gravity up away from the horse.

In some respects, riding is easier for women because their upper bodies are naturally more balanced for the sport. I think that's why 80 percent of the riders showing today are women.

Don't Overdo It

The squareness of your shoulders must not detract from the rest of your body position. It is very easy for a rider to get "stuck" on one problem instead of working on position in general. This leads to frustration and anger on the part of the rider, as he or she just can't understand why this problem won't go away. It doesn't benefit the horse either. The horse can't figure out why things are so riled upstairs. The horse would like to get some peace and quiet,

There are subtle but distinct differences in the way men and women ride. Notice the difference in body structure, which causes subsequent changes in position.

too, but it can't because it's loping around the arena for the 780th time.

Repetition is not necessarily the key to improving a problem. People tend to try the same exercise over and over in a firm belief that "it's going to work this time." I say, if one thing doesn't work, try something else. Another idea may click better for you; another image may make the difference. In any case, trying different ideas and exercises will give you a more pleasurable practice session, as well as offering some variety for your patient horse.

Riders have a tendency to lean in the direction they are going. They drift to the inside of the arc on turns, and this often causes the horse to drop a lead behind, or not take the lead. The unbalanced rider gets in front of the horse's shoulder and interferes with the leads. That upper body must be very careful to not get in the way.

If you are one of those perching on the front of the horse, analyze why you are doing it. Is it because you're in a hurry? Do you believe that getting forward will automatically assure you of shaving a few tenths of a second off your time?

Timed-event riders constantly adjust their position and balance in order to see top performances from their horses.

Getting forward is not always getting in balance. The key to speed, as well as to performance in other events, is balance. If your upper body is ahead of your hips, you are compromising your ability to balance your horse and influence his movement.

So now you think, "Jockeys get forward, don't they?"

A jockey may be forward, but a good jockey is not ahead of his or her horse. At speed, the horse's center of gravity moves ahead, and the jockey matches that, tucking down his or her upper body to minimize wind resistance and following the horse's head and neck with the hands.

This is not an especially stable position. If the horse checks suddenly, or there is a mishap, it isn't uncommon for the jockey to go flying over the horse's head.

The same happens in other sports to the novice rider who gets ahead of his horse. If you are ahead of your horse, and it decides to quit following you, you are helpless to change things unless you radically change your own position.

Flexibility and stability are two sides of the same coin when it comes to body position. You want to be able to move any part

NO

This position is incorrect for Western horsemanship and pleasure classes. It causes the rider to be off balance in relation to the desired frame of the horse.

This is the desired position for Western horsemanship and pleasure classes. The body is organized and in balance.

YES

independently yet keep the main part of the body in a stable, quiet position.

Western riders tend to twist their upper body and lead with their left shoulder because that is usually their rein hand, and the inclination is to get out and point with it. These riders almost always tend to ride off of the left side of their body and can be very crooked and one-sided.

Work on keeping the shoulders square and even, with the upper arm in line with the body, not out in front. Don't overcompensate by getting those elbows behind the body, either, because that causes major problems as well. It gives the impression that you're about to sit up and crow like a rooster.

Another mistaken compensation is to lean forward with the shoulders to bring the upper arm in line. That is the wrong solution. As discussed earlier, that brings your upper body past the center of gravity.

Your body position responds to the activity you are engaged in at the time. You can change your position and shift the horse's center of gravity at will, but you must never sacrifice your ability to maintain control.

This position is often seen in Western pleasure classes as riders attempt to slow the horse down, losing balance in the process.

NO

There are several reasons for the upper arm to stay in line with the body. When it gets out too far, it becomes stiff and you lose the suppleness of your elbow. If your upper body gets ahead of the horse, all the horse needs to do is check one stride, and it puts you off balance. It's easier to sit a little behind the motion and feel the movement.

The current fad in Western pleasure is to ride way behind the motion, thinking that this will slow down the horse. All this really does is brace the rider in the saddle. The rider becomes ineffective because he or she is no longer in balance. The shoulders must be over the hips.

Exercises to Improve the Use of Your Shoulders and Upper Body

I like to use the following exercises for the shoulders and upper body:

1. Trot with your hands off the reins (either on a longe line or in a round pen), circling one arm forward and one arm backward, windmill fashion.
2. Go around the ring in a posting trot, alternately swinging your arms out in front of you with each beat of the trot. Right arm up, left arm up, and so forth. Again, do not hold the reins.

In the past, riders were taught to clamp their elbows to the body by putting a dollar bill there (today we'd use a Master Card). However, I do not recommend this exercise. The clamp effect takes all the suppleness and feel out of your arm and hand. The flow in the horse's movement is gone. It can be argued that this clamping imitates a bitting rig and therefore ought to put the horse in a correct frame. What it actually does is let the horse move around on its front end. Frame is generated from the hindquarters, and they are controlled by the legs and seat, not the hands. You also have to remember that the horse who is wearing a bitting rig is not packing significant weight. Add the bulk of a rider who is moving about in the saddle and you have changed the equation significantly.

Doing exercises with the horse in the round corral or on the longe line enables you to work freely without having to guide the horse.

I like to compare this to when you were a kid playing in the pool, having camel fights. Remember those? There would be mock battles with people piggy-backed on other people's shoulders. A "camel" who had a good rider had a much better chance of staying upright and perhaps winning the match. In contrast, the camel rider who reached too far to one side or did too much wild weight shifting just might tip his or her camel over, and all would get a ducking. Similarly, a horse who is unable to balance the rider properly, can end up getting equally frustrated.

Here are some good exercises for the lower back:

1. Ride with no reins either in a round corral or on the longe line with your arms held in airplane position. Rotate your upper body left and right in time with your horse's trot or lope. Make frequent changes of direction.
2. Vary the first exercise by clasping your arms behind your head as you continue to rotate your upper body back and forth over the pelvis, your pivot point.
3. After you have mastered the second exercise, further vary the exercise by alternately reaching over and touch your opposite toe. (Try this exercise initially at a standstill.)

The upper body organization does more than just produce a pretty rider. It helps create a soft, effective rider.

Resistance-free riding is the ability to execute the fundamentals. Be prepared to cover every detail. Excellence in horsemanship is never an accident.

CASE STUDY 5623: *Ken is a professional horse trainer who starts a lot of colts. He is pretty successful at it. He gets them going fairly well in both directions and at all three gaits, but he runs into trouble when he starts working on stops. His young horses just don't break at the loin and make those long slides you like to see. Instead they're propping into their stops, and it's almost painful to watch.*

The first clue to what's happening to Ken's colts is their stiff, resistant behavior.

Stretching exercises such as toe touches can really improve your ability to use your back.

Fencing a horse introduces it to the proper way to adjust its balance and get down behind. Riders must be extremely supple and soft in their own back to allow this to occur.

When a horse starts getting stiff and bounces into its stops I go back and look at the softness of the rider's lower back. You want the horse to get down into the ground and use himself in a slide. It is a common tendency for a rider to make his or her back rigid in an effort to force the horse down. The rider will tighten his or her body and lean back, creating a force the horse resists.

The first thing that happens to any horse when you don't have a lot of upper body flexibility, is that it gets frustrated. Your body isn't cooperating with its own. A young horse will just sour and quit you instead.

Try trotting the colt up to the fence, keeping your back very soft and letting the fence stop the horse.

> **When resistance-free riders bump their head often enough, eventually they learn to duck.**

4

❀ ❀ ❀

The Importance
of Hands

The consensus in most riding books is that the hands play only a small role in good riding, that the seat and the legs do the bulk of the work. I don't think the hands get enough credit.

I believe the role they play contributes about 40 percent because they create attitude, and through those hands comes a tremendous amount of confidence. They can relax the horse when they are slow and quiet, or they can cause the horse to change its attitude and develop behavior problems.

Look at how the forearm extends through the wrist and fingers, giving you a direct feel to the horse's mouth. The hand is no more than a continuation of your arm, and using your hands is like putting your fingers in the horse's mouth. The bit is totally operated by the hand, and the severity of the bit is determined by the use of the hand.

Great riders and drivers all develop touch and feel in the

This is the correct hand position when using romal reins. The rein hand should be kept vertical, as though you were holding an ice cream cone. The other hand rests lightly on the thigh.

This is the way to hold Western split reins.

fingers. They hold the reins in their fingers in a relaxed but firm manner, just as you would hold a pencil. That doesn't mean they hold their fingers in the same position, but at the same degree of tension.

Experiment with that right now. Sign your name holding the pencil in the normal way. Now clench your fingers in a fist and try signing your name. See the difference?

The fist lacks finesse. The hand is like a laser beam. It can destroy and deaden the mouth, or it can heal the mouth. In good riders, the hands and fingers are constantly active. They are continually shortening and lengthening the reins and signaling the horse.

Their hand motions are always slight and discreet. You don't want to look as though you are pulling salt-water taffy as you trot down the rail.

When your upper body is in harmony with your hand, you are preparing the horse and continually giving him confidence. Your hands must be slow and quiet for this to work and your wrist must be straight. When the wrist is bent, the tendons lose their flexibility and are unable to follow the horse.

There are many joints in the fingers and hand. It's like a little computer, with each key representing something different. The more you practice, the better you will be able to manipulate the computer.

Is the Horse on the Bit or in the Bridle?

A good rider knows the difference between having a horse on the bit or in the bridle. When a horse is in the bridle, the horse is working on a slack rein, carrying itself in balance just a little behind the bit, the poll and body soft. The horse's shoulders are lifted up and its back is rounded as the horse engages its hocks well underneath its body. A horse on the bit is balancing itself on the bit, rather than within its own frame. As a hunter-jumper rider goes over a fence, the horse is on the bit. A driving horse needs to be on the bit. Galloping racehorses are on the bit. Slacken the reins on any of these horses and they fall apart.

A hand yield is an important tool for getting a horse on the bit or in the bridle. Stop your horse and ask it to step backward by pulling on the left rein. The left foreleg and shoulder should move.

The hand yield is a means of teaching the horse to soften and give when asked.

YES

An excessive hand yield teaches the horse to break at the third vertebra and yield incorrectly, instead of softening at the poll.

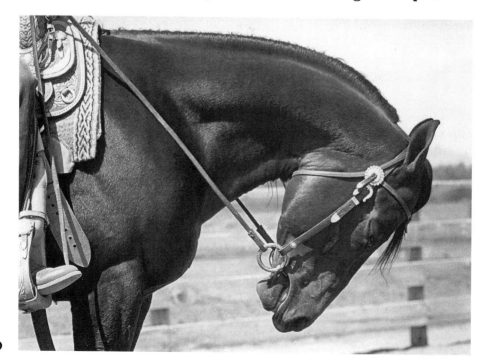

NO

Now release the left rein and pull on the right, asking for the right shoulder to yield and move backward. This is a hand yield. The hand yield creates obedience and suppleness as the horse breaks and softens in the poll. When the horse gives to the hand, the horse is able to use its shoulders and body for balance.

Your hands must be soft and flexible, not harsh and pulling. If your hands are cold, stiff, and unforgiving, you teach the horse to break at the third vertebra. The horse ends up with most of its weight on the forehand, a major difficulty. The rider who develops feel and touch will best be able to utilize the hand yield.

When I was a kid, we rode patterns using single strands of horse hair as reins. We gradually got to where we could do more and more of the pattern before the horse hair broke. That's a little extreme, but it conveys the idea of the lightness you want.

Ways to Improve the Use of Your Hands

In resistance-free riding, I like to have a rider on the longe line with no hands for ninety days before he or she begins using the reins.

After that stage, one of the first things I do, once the rider has established a seat, is put him or her on a light horse to learn the correct feel, the way things ought to be. I think of it as plucking a carrot out of the ground, that lightness of feel. I think it's a mistake for an instructor to use a horse who is heavy in the bridle for teaching. If a rider learns on a heavy horse, he or she will never learn to feel, but instead will pull.

One way to practice feel is to take two chairs and hang a bridle on one. You can do this in the comfort of your living room. Straddle the second chair and practice the feel of taking up and loosening the contact.

You also can practice feel on the ground with a friend. Stand behind another person and have that person move his or her arms back and forth, as if power walking. Holding your friend's shoulders, alternately squeeze each shoulder as that arm comes back. Pretend you are squeezing a sponge.

Notice that this slight pull is relaxing to the person in front. If you do it wrong, squeezing and pulling on the shoulder as the arm beneath it moves forward, your "horse" will become uncomfortable. The wrong thing to do would be to squeeze your right hand at the

You can improve your horse's flexibility by asking the horse to bend its head around as far as possible on both sides. This exercise is done at a standstill so that the horse cannot evade the aids and to help stabilize its balance.

same time as your friend's right arm moves forward. You want to squeeze the opposite shoulder from the moving arm. This exercise gives the person standing behind a sense of how it should feel to follow the rhythm of the horse's front footfalls with the hands.

Another good drill is to sit on your horse and ask it to give to one side or the other, just moving its head and neck, no other body parts. The real key to making this exercise work is to have the horse keep its ears level. Allowing the horse to tilt its head as the horse stretches to one side teaches it that it can run through its opposite shoulder and evade your control (reiners call this "poking the shoulder out"). This results in a horse who will happily turn its head and keep right on going in the original direction with the rest of its body. This is "rubbernecking," and it is not desirable. Remember that tilted ears are a real red light when you're training horses.

Your goal is to be able to gather the horse at will. This can be practiced at the walk, picking him up and letting him out. To learn the difference between your horse being on the bit or in the bridle, practice loosening the reins and then gathering them up, at the same time asking the horse to give to the left or the right.

Don't forget, one of the greatest gifts you can give your horse are hands that feel and show your horse that you care. Good hands produce soft, light horses.

> **A rider who is taught the wrong skills is a rider who can ruin many good horses. A rider who learns resistance-free riding skills can improve every horse he or she rides.**

5

❀ ❀ ❀

Open Eyes and Narrow Eyes

Correct information equals relaxation and confidence. Compare your eyes to a computer. They collect information that tells the body what to do, such as squeeze the right leg to straighten the horse, or adjust the pace a little in order to avoid a slow horse up ahead, or otherwise deal with what's happening. The rider can use the information from his or her eyes to plan ahead for a good ride.

I think of the two eye "positions" as open eyes and narrow eyes. In open-eye mode, the rider is scanning the entire vicinity and aware of everything that goes on within his or her field of vision. In narrow-eye mode, the rider is tightly focused on one thing, such as the horse's ears, which is often unproductive.

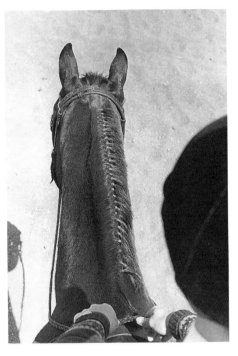

NO

YES

Narrow eyes can limit your view to an area no larger than this. This narrow concentration prevents you from reacting and responding to your surroundings and your fellow riders.

By looking to the horizon, open eyes keep you informed of everything that takes place—and keep you more relaxed.

The Eyes Have It

The open-eyed rider in a rail class plans where he or she is going and stays out of trouble, looking up at all times. This rider stays in the clear and has a good ride instead of being trapped in a cluster of horses.

In horsemanship and dressage classes, the open-eyed rider can see the markers for making transitions. Open-eyed riders in classes over fences perceive the entire course as a whole and judge their ride much better.

The open-eyed reiner knows the distance from the walls, and where the good spots are. Ten feet in one direction or the other can make a big difference. Being aware doesn't mean staring at the marker (that would be narrow eyes), but merely being conscious of it.

The open-eyed endurance rider knows where he or she is going and what sort of trail is coming. This rider has to use open eyes to avoid missing the trail ribbons and getting lost.

The show trail rider uses open eyes to judge position and movement through obstacles. He or she must be able to determine exactly how to position the horse in order to get a clean go.

Cattle-event riders have the difficult task of reading their stock. If the cow raises its head, that means something, and the sharp, open-eyed rider can anticipate what's going to happen, just as if he or she were reading a script. If the rider misses that clue, he or she

In working cow horse classes, you need to have total awareness of the entire ring to demonstrate complete control of the cow. Here, the rider finishes the final circle in the center of the arena and in complete control.

won't read the cow right, and might lose the animal—and the contest.

The timed-event rider needs open eyes to know his or her exact position on course and how to maneuver cleanly. I could go on and on about the importance of good, "open" eyes in riding. If you can't use your eyes well, you're in trouble.

Things go wrong when your eye computer shuts down and you stare at your horse's ears or the ground. I've seen people get so inwardly focused that they literally forgot what was happening in the arena. They usually wake up abruptly when they find themselves tailgating another horse or getting cut off on the rail.

Of all eleven world or national shows I've judged, I've never yet had a champion that didn't use his or her eyes to the maximum. In top-drawer competitions, it's not uncommon to see all of the best riders with a good command of this skill. They can ride an entire performance without lowering their eyes even once; they let their body and legs take care of positioning and moving the horse.

When your eyes aren't looking ahead and taking in the world, your computer shuts down. The screen goes blank. It's like being in a whiteout in a snowstorm. When your view is limited, your body stiffens, whatever the situation, whether you're driving a car, a horse, or a snowmobile.

As your tension increases, your responses may slow down. When your eyes aren't giving you total comprehension, you become stiff and insecure. Without the information of what's ahead of you, your body starts to shut down and tighten up. Just like the panicky swimmer you tighten and sink.

Eye Exercises

At my clinics I like to demonstrate the difference between a narrow and an open eye. Try this on your own. Hold up your thumb and focus your eyes hard the thumbnail. That is a narrow eye. You can lose your equilibrium if you freeze your eyes in the narrow position.

Next, hold up your thumb again. Look past your thumb at the surroundings. Now you're seeing total information rather than just one block of information. An open eye perceives your entire surroundings and keeps the brain supplied with feedback.

Another drill that I often use is to stand in the center of a ring and hold up varying numbers of fingers, asking the riders on the rail to constantly call out the numbers. The riders have to make transitions and continue riding their horses effectively while still being aware of what my fingers are doing.

I also like to have show riders look for different people in the stands, or trees, or lights, continually changing their focus. If they're not keeping their eyes up and looking around, getting information, it's the quickest way in the world to stiffen up.

I find that one of the biggest problems for the novice rider is that the second he or she gets a little bit scared, whether of a strange horse or because of the importance of a competition, his or her body automatically freezes. If you don't believe this, look off the top of a thirty-story building. Your body automatically tightens and freezes.

This natural reaction is one that you must learn to control, or it will stop you. Be aware of that freezing feeling or shakiness. When you sense it coming on, control it by looking up and around as you continue practicing, circling, and stopping.

The skier who looks outward and down the mountain is going to be better able to deal with the slope than the skier who freezes and stares down at the tips of his skies. In the same way the rider who looks up will give his or her computer correct information, thus creating relaxation and confidence.

> **The rider who can make the hard things look easy is a resistance-free rider.**

CASE STUDY 9324: Anne is a young professional in her thirties, showing her horse at her first regional show. She's been successful at the local level, and now she's attending her first major breed show, hoping to earn some points toward her horse's Register of Merit. As she practices in the warmup ring in heavy traffic, she has no problems. The horse is listening and things are in perfect harmony.

As soon as she enters the ring, however, a snowball of trouble starts rolling down the hill. The atmosphere of the show ring is completely different. It's like riding into a big noisy steam bath. To top it off, it's one of those arenas where the audience sits above the arena, giving the whole place a bullring atmosphere. People are making an incredible amount of racket.

She freezes into a rigid pose, staring at her horse's ears because they're something familiar and nonthreatening. The horse feels her literally stop riding and begins to lose his frame. His back drops and his poll comes up. Just at the very moment that she ought to be making a good first impression, she looks her worst. The judge dismisses her mentally and looks at the next horse and rider.

Like this rider, we've all suffered from stage fright. Let's analyze what happened and why.

Out in the warm-up ring, a comfortable, quiet place compared to the show arena, Anne was using her eyes very well, looking up and around, visiting with her friends, watching out for other horses and the inevitable trainers on foot, making sure she didn't run over anyone.

The moment she passed through the gate into the arena, however, she stopped looking around at the world and started staring at her horse's ears. At this point she was just as effective a rider as a store mannequin. She could have given a mannequin lessons on how to be rigid.

Part of the solution for this problem is practice and mileage. Anne needs to get into the ring as much as possible until it's just as comfortable as her living room at home.

The other key to the problem is the use of her eyes. If she hadn't frozen into "narrow eyes," she might have been able to cope with her stage fright and gone right back to work. She would have become more confident and relaxed with correct eye usage—"open eyes"—which would have given her complete awareness of the entire arena.

Anne must remember that she can use her eyes well. She had to use her eyes out in the warm-up arena, or she would have crashed into other horses. The fear of entering the ring in front of the judge and the audience caused her to drop her eyes.

The time that you really need to use your eyes to vacuum in information is when you enter the ring, to avoid riding into a bad spot. The judge's first look at you must show you doing your best.

You aren't doing your best if you're just about to collide with a horse who is already on the rail, or if you are riding right straight over a piece of litter that is sure to distract your horse from its job. You've got to be aware of what's happening all around you. If someone else is having trouble with his or her horse, give them plenty of room and keep right on showing.

Riding in the warm-up ring is like sitting in a classroom at school, comfortable and relaxed. Riding in the show ring is like going up in front of your classmates to give a speech. Now you're tense and worried. Showing horses is no different. You have to get used to being in control of the situation so you can respond correctly. You have to use your eyes correctly and take in all the available information, making it possible for your body to follow through with the correct movements and cues for the benefit of your horse.

6

❀ ❀ ❀

Breathing and Relaxation

The ability to stay relaxed is one of the common traits of top competitors. One of the ways these riders stay relaxed is by breathing properly. Breathing is to your brain as fuel is to a car. Without it, you get tight and can't think effectively.

What almost always happens to a rider when a horse stumbles or shies? When a young horse under saddle bucks? Or when a nervous rider enters the show ring?

The rider stops breathing—holds his or her breath and gets scared. If someone grabs you suddenly from behind, you hold your breath.

The next time something scares you, like a backfire from a car, notice what happens to your breathing. You are naturally inclined to hold your breath.

Hold your breath for ninety seconds and notice how rigid and tight you have become at the end of that time. When you are under

NO

Holding your breath while riding creates tension in both the horse and you.

stress, you need to *make* yourself breathe. Inhale, exhale. Get to know what situations cause you to hold your breath and prepare for them by breathing deeply and clearing your head.

To me that upper body tension is like a balloon ready to pop. Let the air out and out and out until the balloon softens. That's sort of what happens when you learn to breathe under stress.

Again, the natural rider breathes automatically. The majority of riders, however, must learn to breathe off that upper third of the body, filling the lungs. Not only does breathing encourage relaxation, it brings the upper body up off the hips, giving you a correct squareness of posture with a centered feel.

A lot of race walkers breathe off the upper part of their lungs throughout a long race. Without ever inhaling all the way, they keep their upper body up off their hips for freedom of movement. Doing this while you ride allows you to sit lightly on the horse. It also seems to help develop feel. Riders will straighten their back and shoulders just thinking about it.

I spent years trying to teach upper-body organization by asking riders to lift the right shoulder, pull the tummy in, and so forth. All of these orders would actually bring the rider out of position because moving one body part always disrupted the position of another.

Notice what a difference just taking a deep breath can make to your overall body position.

YES

The easiest way to achieve the correct posture is to fill your lungs with air and only breathe out with the upper third. This gives a wonderful straight back, square shoulders and a head position that lets the eyes look around and focus like a computer.

I want to see my students breathing in cadence with their horses' gaits. For example, at the jog, the riders ought to be breathing in a regular, systematic rhythm. This consistency also enables the horse to become more consistent.

Exercises for Better Breathing

The following exercises help develop relaxed breathing patterns:

1. Ride in a posting trot, a two-beat gait, inhaling and exhaling with every other rise and sit.
2. When you have mastered the first exercise, try doing it at a lope in a circle, choosing to exhale or inhale on either the first or the third beat of the canter.

Watch other riders and breathe with them. Determine what you must do in order to improve yourself. Notice that problems begin when riders stop breathing correctly and start holding their breath instead. See how this reflects itself in tension throughout horse and rider.

Resistance-free riders realize that there is a destiny that brings harmony to each horse and rider. No one goes his or her way alone.

CASE STUDY 4022: *Kay is a semi-professional and has ridden all her life, showing successfully over fences, working cattle, showing pleasure horses, you name it. However, when she rides a young horse, she always has trouble.*

She always longes these young horses before she rides them to take the edge off and hopefully assure that she will have a quiet ride. Today she's got a little bay that is not putting a foot wrong out there on the line. He's listening to her voice cues and performing like an old trooper, so she brings him to the center of the arena and gets ready to ride.

She even has someone hold his head while she mounts. Picking up her right stirrup, she settles stiffly down in the saddle and lets out a big sigh of relief when the horse doesn't move.

Now she moves out to the rail. Her helper watches for a moment, then returns to his own chores. Everything is going beautifully, and Kay begins to think that this will be the horse to break the pattern.

Suddenly there is a loud clatter out in the aisle as somebody's horse pulls back in the crossties and flips over. Kay doesn't even think as she snatches at the reins, bringing them almost to her chin, and wraps her legs tightly around the horse in a death grip. While doing all this she sucks in a deep breath of panic and holds it.

Though she isn't thinking, the horse is, and he suddenly believes that he is in mortal danger. He ignores the pain in his mouth and bolts down the rail, oblivious to his rider and all of his surroundings. Kay is clinging to the saddle horn and has absolutely no control of herself or the horse.

Let's see what is happening here.

One indicator that Kay's holding her breath is that she has no trouble on a broke horse, where she has confidence. The moment she climbs on a colt, she gets tight and stops breathing. The problem gets worse and worse because she gets tighter and tighter, and this especially bothers a young horse, who doesn't yet have any confidence in the rider.

The tense rider grabs with the leg and overcues with leg or hand aids, and the quickness scares the horse even more, making it tighter, which in turn makes the rider tighter. Kay should work on her breathing, both on and off the horse.

Young horses are especially sensitive to a rider's stiffness or softness. You can get a young horse to buck you off just by getting nervous and clamping your legs around its barrel.

Resistance-free riding enables riders to know what to remember from the past, what to enjoy in the present, and what to plan for in the future.

7

❀ ❀ ❀

Both Sides Should Be Your Good Side

You must learn to ride off of both sides of your body for maximum movement of the horse. In addition, you must have a stable seat before you can have good hands. But before you can achieve these desirable goals, you must identify your weak areas. Let's start by identifying the weaker side.

Stand on two scales. Let's say you weigh 100 pounds on each scale, or 200 pounds together. If your body isn't aligned, the scales won't be equal. Shifting the upper body or the hips even an inch or two in one direction or the other can result in 10 to 15 pounds of differential on the scales.

If a horse can feel a fly on its flank, the horse can certainly feel these weight shifts. Standing on two scales begins to teach you how radically even a small motion can affect your horse's balance.

You must ride from your center for power. Athletes use their body for power, not just their arms or legs. A quarterback wouldn't

Riders need to use both sides of their bodies for patterns and courses that require turns in both directions.

get a very long throw with just arm power. Instead the quarterback rocks back and brings the entire body into the throw, gaining distance and momentum.

The tough tennis player does the same thing. A number of players grunt as they make their shots. These grunts help them use the power and strength of their diaphragms and centers in reversing the direction of that speeding ball. You can experiment with this for yourself.

You might wish to try swatting a tennis ball, or you can just throw a ball, or a pebble, or a clod. Try different types of throws. Do several with just your arm. These throws aren't going to be as impressive as the ones you achieve when you put your body into the throw.

Rotate your shoulders back and really hurl your upper body in a rotary motion. Discus throwers and shot putters are good examples of how you can really get your body into the throw. See what sort of results you're getting compared with those first tosses.

Now throw in a good "Grrrrrr!" as you throw with your body. Any good grunt, snarl, or "deep" noise will cause you to push outward with the front of your body and improve your posture. You become more aware of your center.

Stop grunting. Your stomach sags back down and inward, depending on your individual conformation. You may even slouch a little compared to your previous position. Now you are not using any of your center.

Do you get a better throw when you are actively growling and centering, or when you are sloppy and soft? Which position would be better for responding to the sudden movements of an opposing player or a reining horse?

Good ropers learn to throw from their center, even if they aren't consciously aware of it.

This doesn't mean that you ought to go out and growl at your horse. Once you learn that growl feeling, you can create it without making a sound.

The next step with the growl feeling is to do several short silent growls instead of one long, drawn-out growl. Repetitions require that you breathe. The dynamics of your breathing will vary according to what you are doing in your riding. For example, a dressage rider who is actively driving for an extended trot is going to be pushing further forward with the belly and working much harder than a Western pleasure rider.

Being One-sided Can Cost You Success

Many riders have one bad direction. Their horse is a totally different animal when it reverses.

Eighty percent of barrel horses turn better to the left because the riders tend to be better in that direction. In contrast, the horses have far more difficulty with their right turns. This can cost you fractions of a second that can make a real difference in placing.

The reiner is also affected by being one-sided. The horse who is fluid to one side may make a rough change to the other side and be relatively unbalanced.

You must be balanced forward and back as well as from side to side. It's really easy to determine whether you are balanced as you ride. If your horse disappeared from beneath you, would you land on your feet? Would you stay on your feet, or topple backward? Or would you tip forward and hit the dirt?

It is extremely common to see riders with their legs out in front of their body in a chair seat. Western and saddle-seat riders tend to brace with a rigid knee, especially when out of balance or trying to ride a horse who is not particularly well trained. They're trying to solve their problems with the bit instead of their seat and leg.

In response to this intense backward motion, the horse loses its brilliance, pins its ears, or otherwise expresses its discomfort. A horse who can still turn in a good performance while packing a rider in this rigid position is truly a champion.

In this back-seat position, the rider feels every jounce and jostle. The lower back absorbs a lot of the movement, and this is not always a pleasant situation.

Exercises That Teach You to Use
Both Sides Well

When I was in Germany, the riders talked a great deal about the "chocolate side" of the rider, referring to the good or strong side. I feel that you have to determine which is your weak side and make a serious commitment to working on it. The following drills develop both sides of a rider:

1. Determine which side is your weak side, then drop the stirrup on that side. Without the support of the stirrup, you must bring yourself into balance.
2. Trot your horse with one hand held straight out in front of you alternating hands with each stride of the horse. This drill, which I call the scissor drill, can also be done with both hands held out in a "sleepwalker" pose.
3. Swing a rope with your weak arm. Try to swing the rope around once with each canter or lope stride in a steady rhythm. This exercise both helps one-sided riders and improves rhythm.

You have to fail before you can win. Take tennis for example. If you have a bad backhand, your opponent is going to play to that weakness and score like a thief. Sometimes you have to get beaten before you can determine your weaknesses and correct them.

I find that for those of us who are one-sided (which is a majority of the population), it is helpful to do some common sports using the weak hand. For example, if you play tennis using your right hand, try a few sets using your left hand. (It's also a great way to handicap yourself!)

Try riding your bike one-handed, using your weakest hand. Or if you ski, try skiing with a single pole on your weak side.

If you are not sports-inclined, just juggling a ball with your weak hand, throwing it a few inches into the air again and again, will help tune up your reflexes and coordination to improve your use of that weak side.

Many riders have one leg longer than the other. You should determine whether this is the situation for you, and compensate accordingly. Mild forms of physical therapy might help you. Sometimes something as simple as wearing an extra sock on your short side or adding an extra insole will help even things out.

NO

YES

If the horse disappeared, would this rider land on her feet?

This rider would be able to stand up if her horse disappeared. She is in a position that is athletic and adaptable to any movement of the horse.

The scissor drill helps riders with their rhythm and timing.

You can change the body you were born with to a certain degree. Naturally, you can't make major changes, like growing from five feet to six feet tall, but you can adjust the little things that can make a big difference. (See the case study on pages 97 and 98 for an illustration of this.)

Treat your horse as if it were a world champion, and you will help your horse follow the road map to becoming one.

8

❀ ❀ ❀

Preparatory Commands

We've all seen the horse-and-rider combination that does every move without visible effort. The timing is right on, the flow is there, the cues are invisible, and you can't find a significant fault.

Put another rider on the same horse and you might have an entirely different result. You may see that willing, cooperative horse go on the muscle, scotching and holding back, his jaw rigid.

The difference is preparatory commands. The first rider was warning the horse of every upcoming transition and exercise by giving a little cue that alerted the horse to be ready. The second rider was just surprising the horse with commands, with no thought as to getting the horse ready or setting it up to perform well.

In the show ring, the riders who use preparatory commands will be head and shoulders above the rest in the results they achieve. They will be able to have great rides on any given day because they can prepare their horses and ride with total harmony.

You can see it elsewhere as well. You've probably seen people

Preparatory commands are an essential part of good horsemanship. This sliding stop is a classic example, showing a horse who is prepared beforehand for the stop.

on trail rides or cattle drives who spend all day in the saddle. You can easily pick out the ones who have had a hard day of it. Their horses are still jigging and tossing their heads, and you can see a lot of sweat on the reins and the horse's neck and sides. The riders look equally uncomfortable. Their jaws are set, their faces grim, and they're getting pretty impatient with Old Paint. When a cow makes a break, they jerk the reins against the horse's neck, pulling so hard on the outside rein that the horse tilts his head to the outside of the turn. These riders turn a simple cow capture into a major battle. The owner of the cattle is losing money because the stock loses weight from all the chousing.

In contrast there are always a few riders whose horses in the afternoon are still fresh, fairly clean, and as quiet as they were in the morning. If one of these hands goes after a stray, it's done quietly with only light reining. The horse is soon heading the cow, and neither of them has broken from a jog. These true riders still have a lot of horse left after long trail rides. While they may be tired, they're not aching from all the bouncing.

The main difference between these two types of rider is technique. Not only does the quiet rider have better riding skills, but this rider also telegraphs his or her thoughts to the horse ahead of time. He or she communicates with the horse in a whisper, not a shout, and never utters an unkind word against the horse. The other rider is likely to gallop back to the herd, yank his or her horse to a hard stop on the forehand, and yell, "Burro!"

A rodeo offers an ideal opportunity to watch good and bad communication. Lots of times there will be at least one horse who is used by several ropers or bulldoggers. Watch this horse's attitude under the different riders. Under one the horse may be quiet and steady, ready to do its job. The next rider may seem to be on a completely different animal as the horse responds to the rider's differing skills and requests. The horse hasn't changed from one rider to the next; the horse still knows its job perfectly, or these contestants wouldn't want to ride it. The only thing that changes is the rider and how he or she tunes into the horse—or doesn't.

Preparatory Commands Get You Ready

Preparatory commands are the equivalent of yellow lights. If there were no yellow lights, and traffic simply had to slam on the brakes without warning when a light turned red, wouldn't you be a little nervous at intersections? With the yellow light, you have time to slow down or speed up and get through the intersection before the light is red.

Think about the conductor of an orchestra. Before the music begins, he or she picks up the baton and gains the attention of the musicians. You have to gain the attention of your horse before you can begin.

Watch how good riders prepare their horses before they ask for a movement. They look in the direction they're going before cueing the horse. In the warm-up ring, they make all their movements slowly and precisely, using a lot of upper body motion in their circles, giving their horses confidence before going into the ring. Every cue is exaggerated during warm-up. These horses then go into the ring and perform.

Preparatory commands build confidence and relaxation in your horse.

Whatever the sport, whether it's working cattle or running barrels, a rider who rides with deliberation and doesn't get upset or excited will get the most from his or her horse.

You can practice preparatory commands at home without your horse. Work with another person, taking turns giving each other one-word commands.

"Jump."

"Turn."

Notice how one-word commands tend to result in jerky motions. Now try giving commands in sentences.

"Get ready to jump. Jump now."

"Prepare to turn left. Turn left now."

There's quite a difference in the response you get. Instead of an abrupt move, it's a smooth action.

Break down the actions that result in various movements from the horse. For example, to go from a four-beat walk to a jog, the Western rider tends to just haul off and kick the horse in the ribs or apply a clamping leg. The result is like grabbing your toothpaste in the middle of the tube.

The better rider prepares his or her horse. The rider raises his or her hand slightly, lifts the chin and chest a bit, and lightly taps the lower leg against the horse's side in time with its footfalls. The horse is alerted to the upcoming transition by the lifting of the rein, followed by the lifting of the rider's chest. The next cue is that bumping with the leg, keyed into the horse's leg motion, left leg and left hind, and so forth. The horse then gives a smooth transition from walk to jog.

When the rider goes from walk to lope, the upper body shifts a little weight to the outside stirrup, the chin and chest rise slightly, and as the rider starts to lift his or her hand and move it to the outside, tightening the inside rein, the horse lightens the inside shoulder and rises into a departure. The rider squeezes with that outside weighted stirrup. The inside leg is held at the cinch, supporting the horse's shoulder. The finished horse will respond to the lift of the chin and upper body to prepare for the lope, and then only the slightest movement of the rider's hand will be necessary. The colt may require that its rider lift the hand several inches in the early part of training to make the cue more noticeable.

Polished to the utmost, the outside aids become a mere tightening of the lower leg, and the cues become nearly invisible.

A horse can be turned in the same manner in which you ski a turn. You release a little with the inside leg and let the horse turn in the direction you wish to go, letting your body weight stay slightly to the outside of the arc. With a little more leg or a little more rein, the horse moves into a circle or on a straight line.

Flying Changes with Preparatory Commands

Let's look at how flying lead changes work. We'll break down a change from right to left. In lead changes, the horse must keep

This rider is preparing to do a flying change from right to left. First he alerts the horse with preparatory commands as described in the text.

its shoulders and hips in line. On a young horse you always use two hands.

First look to the left. Your upper body then starts to turn in that direction.

Next, pick up the left rein several inches and shift your weight from the left stirrup to the right stirrup, stepping lightly. As you do

In this stride, the horse begins to adjust its balance to make the lead change, hind leg first.

The lead change is complete, and the horse is in good balance, ready for the next change, and still relaxed.

that, the right leg pushes the horse's hip to the left, and the horse changes leads, hind legs first, in the correct manner. To do the changes in the other direction, just reverse the instructions.

Don't make big motions with your upper body and try to throw the horse into its changes. The result of using too much upper body movement is that you actually hold the horse's shoulder down and prevent the horse from changing leads. The horse will be too busy trying to keep its balance to figure out what you're asking. Flying changes aren't done with force if they're done well.

Stopping with Preparatory Commands

In stops, the upper body in the seated position prepares the horse. On a young horse, you stop your upper body movement and come slightly—only slightly—behind the vertical. As the horse becomes more polished, your merely sitting down a little more firmly coupled with a light squeeze of the rein, will give the desired result. As you squeeze your hand, keep it almost stationary, don't just pull back.

For a good stop, rhythm is very important. You begin your cues to stop from the first or third beat of the lope.

The rider prepares the horse for a sliding stop with the initial preparatory commands in the sequence of the lope. The rider's lower back and seatbones drive the horse into the stop; his shoulders are squared and his weight is in his heels.

In response to the preparatory commands, the horse begins to adjust its body position in order to stop smoothly.

The end result is a balanced, correct stop with a relaxed horse and rider able to maximize the amount of slide.

Long-trotting allows horse and rider to increase the amount of engagement and forward impulsion while practicing. Done correctly, it will give the horse more reach from its shoulders and a greater length of stride.

Practice your stops on foot before you try them on a horse. Make short runs on foot and see what your upper body does before you make each stop. You don't lean forward or way back, but you do settle and organize for the stop. That is like your preparatory command for the horse, telling it to get ready, we're about to stop.

Exercises That Improve Your Body Usage

The following exercises help to teach you to use your body to give preparatory commands:

1. On foot, carry a sack of feed around, doing circles and turns. See how your upper body turns in the direction you're going before your feet actually make the turn. This is the same thing you do on your horse for good communication. Turning the body first also slows down the hand, a true advantage because it quiets the horse.
2. Trot your horse, asking it for the longest possible stride. You will have to incline your upper body slightly forward to stay with the movement. Then say whoa, which is step one, sit down, which is step two, and then, pull slightly on the rein. The polished horse will stop with only a tightening of the fingers. The first two steps of the stop command will be all that you really notice.

Resistance-free riders train their horses to always listen before they perform the requested movement.

9

❀　❀　❀

The Ripple Effect

The horse is a very tolerant and kind animal. Just look at what it puts up with from poor riders. Any horse could wipe out the average rider in seconds—but horses don't, because they are basically good-natured creatures.

It's our duty to do our best by them. Even if you are not a natural rider, you can learn to feel and respond to your horse's movements in a manner that will both benefit your horse and enhance your performances.

I use the term "ripple effect" a lot. The ripple effect refers to the feeling of motion and strength coming up from the horse through the rider's body. The ripple effect is generated by the impact of the horse's hooves on the ground, which creates a rebound effect like that of a basketball, only much more subtle. Different gaits have different ripple effects. The walk is the most "ground bound," and the gallop is the most rhythmic because there is a significant period of suspension in the beats. The horse uses this rebound effect to make its own movement easier.

The walk requires the horse to physically lift each leg and put it down. The gait's lack of speed and spring keeps the horse's legs from creating much of a rebound effect.

At the trot, the horse bounces from one pair of legs to the other, with a little period of suspension in between. The horse can derive a "coasting" effect from the rebound. It's like when you are running downhill. Once you get started, you can keep going with little effort.

You can really see the ripple effect in the kangaroo. It is almost effortless for a kangaroo to bound along, but very awkward for it to try and walk with individual steps. In contrast, when a kangaroo jumps, its long hind legs compress during the landing from each leap and launch the animal into the next.

The horse operates in a similar manner, but not nearly as efficiently. Fortunately, the horse's differences make it a much softer animal to ride than the kangaroo. (Kangaroo Western Pleasure?)

I like to describe the ripple effect as a soft vibration, like the ripples you see when you throw a pebble into a pond. The ripples go from the center of the impact outward to the shore.

A rider who understands the ripple effect and how to use it will be able to get on any horse and put it in a correct frame. The rider will be able to get the most out of the horse. Mastering the ripple effect will give you a command of the rhythm and timing necessary to achieve maximum performance.

Feel the Ripple Effect

To get an idea of how the ripple effect feels, stand on the ground and stamp one foot down hard. The vibrations you feel in your body are similar to those generated by the horse, although the horse's vibrations are far more subtle. Try doing this with one and then both arms overhead.

You can feel the vibrations of the foot stamping all the way to your fingertips. Now repeat the experiment while clenching your fist, tightening your elbow, holding your breath, and stiffening your knees and various other body parts. You'll notice that a stiff or rigid area is just like a dam, stopping the flow of the ripple effect. What does this mean to the rider? It means that the stiff rider will lack total suppleness and harmony in following the horse's movement.

With a relaxed body, the flow of the vibration is like that of a waterfall or an electrical current. It transmits freely all the way through the body.

The Ripple Effect Makes a Difference

I first became aware of the ripple effect as a judge, watching hundreds of riders go past me at all gaits. Some of them would be stiff as a board. You could see them loping along, upper body pumping back and forth as though they were on a pogo stick. This is caused by a tight lower back that blocks the ripple effect. The tight lower back also discourages the horse from rounding its own back and moving in the most efficient and attractive manner. When the rider's lower back softens, his or her upper body loses that excess motion and allows the rider to become more in tune with the horse.

Unskilled riders often bounce a lot at the jog trot. This results from tightness in the rider's knees and ankles, which act as shock absorbers in the correct rider. If the lower legs are rigid, the rider is pushed up and away from the horse at every stride. The horse is also getting the worst part of the deal, as a pile driver is landing on the horse's kidneys or withers at every step. Softening the lower legs will allow the motion to be absorbed near its point of origin, and the rider will move as a unit with the horse, instead of jiggling like a loose backpack.

A weak rider will magnify the bumping effect of the jog, and it will be reflected in jarring movement of the rein hand. The strong rider will have independent hands and arms that move as necessary to follow the horse's mouth and are affected little by the body motion below.

Riders who are tight often create horses that pull as a reflex. By exercising the shoulder, the elbow, or the wrist, these riders can improve their feel of the horse and its motion, which will help stop the horse from pulling.

You can always spot the weak riders. They're jogging down the rail looking like woodpeckers. Their chins are poking in and out, their shoulders are coming up and down, and their elbows are flapping like wings. All of this disruptive activity above comes from the weakness of the lower body, which isn't absorbing and using the motion it's receiving from the horse. If the horse is a smooth mover, a rider can get by, but a rough horse will require real riding.

Have you ever driven a car that was out of alignment, or had a crooked frame? How about a bicycle with a twisted frame? If the foundation isn't right, the rest of the structure won't be right, either.

A good rider can make a rough-gaited horse look smooth. Surprisingly enough, it is often easier to do lead changes on a rough-gaited horse because its movement is more active.

The really good rider can fine-tune the ripple effect and adapt it as necessary to improve the horse's performance. It's like the subtleties of the orchestra leader. With the merest wave of the leader's finger or baton, a section of the orchestra is made louder or more quiet, faster or slower, contributing to a complete unit that plays (and finishes) the music together.

The skilled rider needs to know how strong an aid to use, and when to let up on the aid. The rider who lacks an understanding

This simple exercise and its variations can introduce you to the ripple effect on horseback.

of the ripple effect will never know when to say when, so to speak. It's like someone driving a car who only has the accelerator floored or off, with no in between.

A rider can learn feel after he or she identifies the ripple effect and sees its influence on the horse. For example, let's look at a flying change. The rider who prepares for the lead change gathers the energy to move the horse's shoulders and hips over to the side. The rider applies more pressure with his or her leg, the horse makes the change, and the rider then backs off the aid, rewarding the horse for its response.

The novice tends to clamp a leg on the horse and keep on squeezing even after the horse has responded. This creates a dead-sided horse.

I noticed while watching the National Finals Rodeo that all of the team ropers had exceptional rhythm, timing, and energy release. They had to synchronize their movements with their horses and respond to split-second adjustments while making a good run, and it worked. It's a pretty sight when it's right.

Making the Ripple Effect Part of You

One of my favorite exercises to introduce novice riders to the ripple effect is to have a person on the ground, walking beside the mounted novice. The rider extends his or her inside arm and moves it in a circle in rhythm with the walk as the ground person calls out every time the horse's inside hind foot hits the ground.

The ground person may say, "now, now, now," or count, "one, two." The idea is for the rider to begin getting the feeling of when that inside hind leg hits the ground. With the ground person beside the horse, the rider is free to sit in the saddle and just "feel" what is happening, watching the circling arm out of the corner of his or her eye and listening to the ground person. The feedback from both the voice instructions and the circling arm helps the rider correlate what he or she feels with what is happening with the horse. The rider learns to feel the ripple effect without fighting it.

If I have a hyperactive student in a clinic, or one who can't focus and concentrate long enough to accomplish anything, I ask him or her to dismount and jog alongside the horse. This improves the concentration in the best way: the rider's mind can't wander off the subject. (Naturally you can only do this at the walk and trot.) This

A good ground person can be invaluable in helping you learn to identify and use the ripple effect. Here the ground person helps the rider with the rhythm of the footfalls.

exercise is especially useful for the rider who tends to constantly change speed instead of maintaining a steady rhythm.

Another exercise to help the rider feel the ripple effect is to have the rider on the horse, extending one arm upward as though to screw a light bulb into a ceiling socket. I ask riders doing this exercise to close their eyes, then tell me when they feel that ripple effect surging through their stirrup or seatbone on the side with the raised arm (this exercise should be done in a longe line or in a round pen). This exercise easily identifies the rider's stronger side. I have observed that 40 percent of the "pretty good" riders, those who are competent but can't quite break through into being world-class riders, are distinctively one-sided in their riding. Their good side is developed far more than their weak side.

I ask these one-sided riders to trot past me with their right hand extended in the "light bulb position," and have them say repeatedly "now" whenever they think their horse's right hind foot is hitting the ground. Usually riders find doing this exercise on one side, often the right, very easy. They'll call the horse's footfall perfectly every time. Next I have them reverse, change arms, and repeat the exercise. Almost inevitably they'll still call out "now" when the horse's right hind foot hits, instead of correctly identifying the fall of the left foot.

Think of the rhythm section of a marching band. The band can move around without the drums, but the band members march together a lot better when the drums are beating. People have a natural tendency to pick up that rhythm and get in step. The point of the above exercises is to help the one-sided rider get in step. Without that synchronization, the rider cannot generate real power in the horse's movement, and his or her timing will very likely be off, because timing is generated through rhythm.

To improve a rider's foundation, there is nothing better than longe-line work. Classical riding traditionally requires a rider to do months of work on the longe line before he or she is allowed to ride independently. This allows the rider's seat to become completely developed without punishing the horse.

One of my most effective longe-line exercises starts with the horse and rider at a standstill. (I recommend that you have the

Exercises on horseback can help you gain an awareness of body position for both you and the horse.

Riding over cavalletti or logs improves the horse and rider's inner balance, as well as helping them develop greater rapport.

ground person hold the horse's head until you know how the animal is going to respond to these activities.) First, I ask the rider to rotate his or her upper body from side to side, keeping the shoulders level and developing the feeling of a well-oiled joint between the ribs and the hips. This also can be done with the rider's arms held straight out in airplane position, or with the hands held straight up in the air, raising the center of gravity as high as possible. After the rider does these exercises at a standstill, I ask him or her to repeat them at all gaits while circling on the longe line. These exercises get the rider to draw down into the horse and really learn to use his or her seat to move with the horse.

Western riders have a tendency to get up off their horse's back and partially stand in their stirrups instead of sitting right down and absorbing the horse's movement. It is very easy for things to get out of whack. In stops, the seat tightens and comes off the horse's back. If the horse moves more quickly, the rider fails to remain in synch and the horse becomes resistant. If the rider is perching in the stirrups, he or she can't follow the horse well. The rider's center of gravity is moving farther and farther from the horse.

A good correction for a rider who doesn't sit down into the horse is to have him or her work in the round corral without a bridle while a second person controls the horse, sending it around at a good pace. The ground person then suddenly steps in front of the horse, causing it to roll back to the inside hard and fast. A few sessions like this will soon have a rider sitting deeply into the horse in order to survive! (This can be done on the longe line as well, but the effect is best with a free horse in the round corral.)

To get a feel for the ripple effect itself, I suggest working over cavalletti or ground rails at all three gaits. The cavalletti cause the horse to exaggerate its footfalls and use its body more, making it easier for you to feel the movement occur. When you can feel the ripple effect, you can follow it.

The rider who understands the ripple effect will learn to use the lower leg and seat to gather the horse and round its back. This is especially important at the three-beat lope, when the horse must be gathered and released between the first and third beats, in time with the gait. The rider will keep his or her horse at an even three-beat lope, never adding a fourth beat. The ripple effect becomes disrupted and out of tune in a four-beat lope; it is like trying to listen to the radio when the station isn't quite tuned in.

Transitions made with the aid of the ripple effect are energetic and precise. Because your timing will be right, your horse will be working with you instead of trying to catch up with a series of surprise commands.

> **The world-champion rider in any event was at one time a beginner.**

CASE STUDY 7541: *Connie has always shown in rail classes but would like to get into individually judged classes like Western riding. Her horse is a great packer who does flying changes easily from right to left, but isn't consistent changing from left to right. He is really responsive and soft to the leg, so Connie can't understand where she's losing the connection.*

She's been practicing lead changes at home for some time now, using buckets and cones as markers. The pattern is fun, but the horse still isn't changing leads like he should. Eight out of ten times he drops a hind lead when making a flying change from left to right.

How can Connie put things together and master her flying changes? Why does her horse tend to drop a hind lead in his flying changes in one direction but not the other? Connie needs to go back to the basics.

First, she needs to develop the feel and rhythm of the ripple effect at the lope. This lets her use her lower leg and her seat to gather the horse to change from behind first. Then, she needs to do a lot of leg yielding in both directions to improve her control of her horse's hindquarters, especially to the poor side. She herself is probably stronger on one side of her body. I would definitely have her do some exercises to improve her coordination and strength.

She says her horse is definitely responsive to the leg on the left side and is very supple and yielding. Many times a rider lets his or her lower leg creep forward, causing the horse to give in the rib cage instead of the hip. By using the leg further back, the rider correctly activates the horse for the change. I suggest that Connie be careful to use her lower leg behind the girth to move her horse's hip, because that's the key to the flying change.

**Never judge those who try and fail,
only those who fail to try.**

10

❀ ❀ ❀

It's All in
Your Mind

Your mind is like a computer. You want to have a fault-free circuit board operating the system. It's your job to make sure that this good circuit board is in charge before you even start working with your horse.

I find that the proper mental attitude helps the resistance-free rider meet the challenges of horse training. I compare horse training to planting a crop. First you cultivate the ground, then you plant the seeds, and then you fertilize and water on a regular basis until the crop is ready. However, the seeds will not grow without sunlight.

For riders, sunlight is the proper mental attitude. When you go out to ride, or to a show, you prepare properly by being bright and optimistic. You can torpedo yourself by being gloomy and waiting for mistakes to happen.

Don't allow the problems you confront in the rest of your life—

I've had a lot of opportunities to observe, to learn, and to teach riders all over the world.

your job, your home, whatever—to leak into your riding life. When you walk through the barn door, you should make a fresh mental start for the day. You must be able to literally blink your way into a good frame of mind. If you punish your horse for the problems other people have inflicted on you that day, or just because you want to take your anger out on something, you're sacrificing a noble relationship with your horse.

I believe that 85 percent of a successful ride is in your mental preparation. If you have that, you have the potential to soar with the eagles.

Accentuate the Positive

When you ride, look for the positive, rather than the negative. What green lights is this horse showing you that you can capitalize on for a better ride? Rehearse your upcoming ride, whether you are schooling or at a show, thinking your way through your turns, stops, and other required movements.   Envision these actions falling perfectly into place, going like clockwork. If you think only about what can go wrong, it's guaranteed that something will. Most horses have open attitudes, and serve as mirrors of their riders. If you want your horse to reflect well on you, then you must give the horse something good to reflect.

If you groom your horse roughly because you're in a bad mood, the horse is going to get tense and uncomfortable. Horses don't like unpredictable behavior. It isn't any fun being a rider's punching bag. If you are patient and forgiving while handling your horse, you'll find that the horse will become a tolerant, quiet animal that is a good friend and partner.

A show rider can mentally rehearse events at home, on the way to the show, or even while waiting for the class to begin. It's been amply proven that mental rehearsal can be nearly as effective as physical practice when preparing for an athletic sport. Use this mental rehearsal period to focus your mind in depth on what you need to do to create the perfect ride. I've often parked my equitation students off in a quiet corner and asked them to describe the perfect ride. They can run it through on their own mental video, or they can watch good riding on a video at home and improve in that fashion.

I've had great success with having riders practice by watching a good video eight to ten times; they've shown marked improvement in their riding skills with absolutely no practice on the horse. I can show a rider a video on lead changes and get more improvement than if I take that same rider out into the arena and give him or her ten private lessons on lead changes.

I used to think that a rider would improve by watching a video of his or her mistakes. That has not proved to be the case. The only thing you learn from watching mistakes is how to make the mistakes. By watching videos of good, correct performances, you will both consciously and unconsciously imitate them.

If you watch good riders, you yourself will improve. That's one of the benefits of riding at a top competitive show barn. You see good riding every day and learn from it. This does not mean that you should watch good riders at a show and psych yourself out that you can't perform as well as Joe Smith. Watch Joe Smith as an equal and note what he does well, and the techniques used. Remain self-assured that you have your own good skills and plan to win.

Practice Being Perfect

Walking through a pattern is good practice. It enables you to rehearse positioning and turning without grinding your horse into the ground. Think as you walk and use the muscles that you would use if you were on horseback.

You often see riders rehearsing a pattern in their mind as they wait to enter the show ring. Their thoughts are turned inward and their hands dart back and forth, fingers twiddling in midair as they imagine their way through the ride.

It can be helpful to develop mental tunnel vision during a ride, directing your mind to ignore the little "negative outlaw," who is always sitting on your shoulder, whispering about the mistakes you're going to make. Instead, knock that little outlaw off your shoulder, go into the ring, and have your best ride. Think to yourself, "I've been practicing hard, I've been taking lessons, I've been doing everything possible to get ready for this moment, and I'm ready!" Plan to have a nice ride, and you'll have one.

After booting the negative outlaw off your shoulder, focus your

Practice on the ground can help you get ready without causing your horse to anticipate or become sour.

You can teach yourself to go on automatic by using a mental mantra or phrase, while letting your horse do its job.

energy on keeping things simple. Don't make your ride any harder than necessary. For example, if you are making flying changes in a Western riding pattern, think, "One, two, three, change; one, two, three, change," and so forth. Don't get overly involved in thinking, "I've got to move the shoulder over, move the hips, squeeze tighter with the outside leg, get more give in the poll, time it right." If you think too much, the ride will suffer. Remember, a show isn't a place for learning skills. If you can't perform the necessary movements automatically at home, you aren't ready to be at a show.

For the barrel racer, your magic phrase might be as simple as "turn and drive, turn and drive." Don't get caught up thinking, "don't drop that shoulder, watch that left ear, keep him bent." The more you complicate matters, the more slowly you will perform in the speed events.

"Block and turn. Block and turn." That's going to sum up action for the cutter. If you get too wound up with wondering about whether that cow's going to back fence, whether your horse is leaking, or whether you remembered to tighten your cinch before you started, you're going to inhibit your ability to show your horse.

Take every opportunity during a competition to get off by yourself. You have to know yourself and know how to focus. Some riders do well when they spend the time between classes gabbing with their friends. Other riders need to retreat into themselves for a few minutes and create the appropriate state of mind. For myself, I find that ten minutes alone with my horse gives me time to visualize that perfect pattern, that flawless run.

Be wary of your fellow competitors. Some of them will play mind games with you, ostensibly stopping to wish you well, then adding, "I hope your mare doesn't drop a hind lead like she did two weeks ago."

By retreating to a quiet area, you can help minimize these interruptions, and should you be disturbed, you will have time to recover your winning attitude. Keep away from those who want to dump negative thoughts into your mind, and ask your coach, your parents, and your friends to limit any last-minute conversation to positive comments.

One of my riders was competing in horsemanship at the American Junior Quarter Horse Association (AJQHA) World Show. She had done extremely well in the preliminaries, and it looked as though she had a lock on the title. Her first ride had gained her a score three points ahead of anyone else.

Then, just before she rode into the finals, her mother tapped her on the knee and pointed out that this pattern was a lot like one at a show where her horse had missed a lead change. With this last negative thought in mind, she rode in—and missed the lead change in the exact same spot. She made the top ten, but that was all. She had to wait two years to win the championship.

Don't let past performances cloud your present. Every time you enter the ring, it's a whole new ride. Don't think about your horse being a little rank or getting a little quick at the lope. Think about what the horse does well and enjoy the ride. You can get more out of your horse, even the average horse, if you ride it as though it were a champion.

Before entering the ring, warm your horse up properly, preparing for a good ride, giving the horse the schooling it needs in order to do its best. Don't try to train your horse in the warm-up ring; just reinforce the movements that need a little polish and get ready to enjoy the ride of your life.

Evaluating Yourself

After the class ends, review your ride and think about where it could have been better. Talk with your coach and work out areas that need improvement or changing in order to achieve a perfect ride. Don't dwell overly long on what went wrong. Just decide what to do and go on from there.

When I was running my own training barn, I had everyone in the place thinking blue ribbons. I was like Vince Lombardi. There was no color but blue in my book. That mental pressure on the riders was counterproductive. I'd end up with only one customer at the year's end—the one who could beat all the others.

There will be many times when you win a class and don't really deserve it. Maybe it was Christmas that day. Maybe you were the only one in a novice class who knew both leads. On the other hand, there will also be many, many times when you don't come out with a ribbon or a trophy, even when your horse was flawless. The judge doesn't always see everything. Or maybe there were many flawless rides in that class. You can't let the ribbon tell you how good or bad you were. Sixth place in a ring full of tough customers means a whole lot more than a blue ribbon over inferior competition. If you get too wrapped up in winning blue ribbons, you'll lose your perspective on what riding is all about.

I changed my barn's emphasis to treating horse showing as a team effort. We all cheered for each other and tried our best to beat another barn, or whatever, and we were all a lot happier. That was great, but we weren't getting the individual rider that I wanted to see, and we weren't developing long-term riders with exceptional skills as well as we were when everyone was out to beat one another. I decided to give the riders individual goals to increase their motivation.

All of these riders knew their abilities and those of their horses.

When the riders left the ring, they could tell me where their good and bad spots had been. I'd ask them to give me a numerical score about how the class went, from one to ten. The rider might say "Six." Or maybe "Ten." But whatever the score, he or she analyzed the performance and saw what went well and what didn't. These riders learned that their toughest competition was themselves.

I also asked these riders to pick out one good thing about their ride. Even with a bad ride, something had to have gone well, and I asked each rider to identify that successful moment. That helped defuse the situation if things went badly. The riders had less tendency to blame the horse for everything.

With this system, my riders were still pleased with wins, less so with other placings; however, they learned something more valuable: to be pleased with a good ride, whatever it was awarded. The capacity to analyze a ride and determine whether it was good, bad, or uneven, and relate the performance to the potential of the horse is what creates long-term horsemen.

The resistance-free rider competes and rides only against himself.

❀　❀　❀

PART TWO

❀　❀　❀

The following chapters deal with specific classes and competitive divisions found in the show ring. They build on the concepts discussed in Part One and are meant to be used to refine performance after the basic elements are achieved.

11

❀　❀　❀

Resistance-free Western Pleasure

In pleasure classes, the rider who truly takes advantage of resistance-free riding techniques can use the ripple effect to the maximum. This rider can get incredible cadence and steadiness from the horse, using his or her legs to frame the horse and to adjust stride as necessary to position the horse well in the ring. This rider can get the horse into the corners with a leg that is forgiving and soft, rather than forcing the horse into place.

This rider is also going to use his or her eyes to best effect. The rider who really has open eyes and good placement in the ring is the one who is going to win most of the classes. He or she is going to be seen by the judge to best advantage. Let's face it—you can't win the class if nobody ever sees you. The rider who doesn't have awareness of the entire ring will ride up on other riders, get covered up on the rail, and not get a clean ride. The narrow-eyed rider runs into traffic and lets other horses come into his or her space.

The resistance-free rider is going to take advantage of preparatory commands. He or she will have schooled the horse to be ready for transitions before they are made. The prepared horse will remain focused on the rider.

When backing up for example, the rider who prepares the horse before actually cueing the back will have an even cadence, as opposed to the rider who just grabs the horse without warning, causing the horse to pop its head up, hollow its back and probably not back at all.

The rider who is mentally prepared can create an attitude of quietness, almost laziness in his or her horse. If the rider feels nervous, he or she can use positive thinking to pick up a little self-confidence and have a good ride. The rider will make good passes and nice transitions in front of the judge because this rider can handle the pressure.

I find that the pleasure rider who uses the ripple effect, open eyes, even breathing, preparatory commands, and a good mental attitude is the one who is going to be superior. He or she will not only win the class, but be in a position to improve almost any horse. This rider will be able to move a novice horse up a notch in skill and get it out of that division in a hurry. On stake night, the five magical keys are going to help him or her get that clean ride that wins.

Breathing is very important to the pleasure rider. Good breathing should be established before you go into the ring. It seems that the time from when you leave the warm-up area to when you enter the show ring is when your nerves really go into overdrive. You get anxious about competing with your peers and being on stage for all the world to see.

As the announcer calls for you to enter the ring, take about five deep breaths before you go in. Make this a habit. It will help you ride more efficiently and make a good first impression on the judge.

You should also make it a point to breathe deeply before transitions and continue to do so during the transition. I like to tell my students, "when you hear the announcer ask for a gait change, take about two deep breaths and then give your horse the aids to do the task." This brief pause also helps keep the horse tuned into your aids instead of working off of the announcer.

Your riding position is very important in the pleasure division. You can either make your horse look outstanding, consistent, and fluid, or you can make the horse seem rough, stiff, and ready to run away. More so than in any other class, the rider needs to be as

Before entering the ring for competition, take five deep breaths.

balanced and organized as possible so that the horse can have maximum purity of gait and movement.

The resistance-free rider must be attuned to keeping his or her horse in balance, neither leaning heavily on the forehand nor excessively light in front. The rider accomplishes this with a subtle combination of leg and hand aids that create collection while maintaining clean movement. A horse gains security from the stability of the rider's seat and legs, and both horse and rider stay better balanced. Their respective equilibriums enhance one another.

You as a rider must be equally strong on both sides of your body. This makes it possible for you to have good rides in both directions, instead of having to hide when working in your weak direction.

The top pleasure prospect has to be a superb mover with a good mental attitude. These outstanding horses can really get your attention. As a judge, you almost can't look away from them. However, the ideal pleasure prospect may not be the same horse you'd look for as a reining prospect. In reining and other action events, athleticism counts for much more than quality of movement.

Do stay up to date when it comes to Western fashions and equipment. Like it or not, the Western division is very fad-oriented and styles come and go as regularly as they do in the nonriding world. Having an out-of-date hat or a shirt that's out of fashion can be a handicap. It may seem silly, but your clothing is part of the overall picture that you are presenting to the judge. What you wear can be an enhancement or a detriment. Try to select colors that compliment you and your horse. There is a complete science to this, and consultants are often called on to help get the right outfit together.

The quality of your equipment should also be top-notch. Avoid extreme styles that will quickly become dated. Some saddles can be brought up to date by modifying their silver; others will need to be replaced. The same goes for bridles and breast collars. Keep an eye on what's happening in the horse magazines to keep abreast of tack and clothing trends.

Your training program should take into account that you and your horse will reach certain peaks and then drop off slightly in between. You can't keep a horse at its peak constantly. It's not like tuning a machine and having it stay put. The same is true for you. Prepare yourself as effectively as you prepare your horse.

Exercises and Practice Tips

Spend at least two twenty-minute sessions weekly practicing resistance-free exercises and drills to keep yourselves polished. In these practice sessions you can use a portable radio or stereo to help you achieve rhythm and cadence in the gaits. You may also wish to school the horse on different surfaces, such as concrete, pavement, or hard ground, to better listen to the footfalls and strive for consistency.

To improve eye use, look at the second corner, in other words, look diagonally toward the corner after the next one you will be riding through. This helps you to ride straight lines and go well into the corners while maintaining control of the horse and having a commanding view of the entire arena. Mentally inventory the position of other horses in the arena and what they are doing. Having a ground person assist you while you perform transitions can help you remember to keep your eyes up.

As a judge, I see lots of good movers in pleasure classes. As a result, it is often the horse with the most fluid transitions that wins. It is important that your horse learns not to make quick transitions.

A personal stereo can really help you establish good rhythm in your riding.

Before you make a transition to a walk, take one deep breath. Before transitions to a jog, take two deep breaths. Before transitions to a lope, take three deep breaths. These breathing techniques should be used both for transitions to a faster gait and those to a slower gait.

The Western horse should feel and accept your leg. Start working on this by moving your leg position at the walk. For example, ask your horse to move its hip over slightly as if to do a lope, but don't allow the horse to lope. Instead, ask the horse to hold that lateral position as the horse travels for a few steps. Then release the leg, which rewards the horse.

A good exercise for keeping a horse light is to lope your horse from corner to corner to corner, stopping the horse in each corner using just upper-body aids. Next, repeat the exercise, but this time when you reach a corner pause and stand for a moment, then pull your horse's nose toward the rail and circle the horse into the corner. That rocks the horse's weight back onto its hind end and lightens its front end. Lope the next side and repeat this exercise in the next corner, and so forth.

Mental preparation can also help your horse improve. Visualize your horse as slowing down and becoming steady in its rhythm, and it will happen. This is especially true when you are going the second direction of the ring.

Riders tend to get uptight when they reverse during the class, and the horses get hot. Riders also tend to get more anxious going in one direction than the other. When they are going in their "weak direction," the riders don't perform as smoothly. Pleasure-horse riders get into trouble by thinking too much. They need to go back to their transitions and break them down into simple one-two-three elements. They need to develop a harmony with their horse so that it feels as though they themselves are doing the transition.

Just before entering the show ring, review your mental videotape and visualize your horse as soft and pliable—like a marshmallow, for example—and keep that amount of softness as you enter the arena. Your horse will become what you envision.

Keep a record of what judges you like and dislike, and notes on what different judges seem to prefer. It's also useful to log in information on show grounds. I like to score both judges and facilities with scores from one to ten.

Periodically, you will need outside help in the form of honest evaluations from instructors, trainers, or friends. Ask them to point out at least two aspects of your performance that are good, plus two that need work.

Remember, you must fail before you can succeed.

Horses must learn how to obey, then whom to obey, then when to obey.

CASE STUDY 3211: *Mike is in his twenties and has just entered college. This is his first year as an amateur. He finds that his Western-pleasure horse gets quicker and stronger as his rides progress. The mare starts out slow and ends up moving like a Kentucky Derby winner by the time Mike's finished. No matter how often he stops and backs her up, or pulls on the reins, the mare gets fast. The horse is still in a snaffle because Mike knows that she isn't ready for the curb bit, until this problem is solved.*

Right away I know Mike's into the horse's face too much; his tight rein indicates he's not trusting her. Any time a rider takes a strong hold of a horse and pulls back to slow the horse down, the horse tends to quicken and fall onto its front end.

This horse needs to go on a slack rein. I would alternate movements and transitions to get her hocks under her. Go from a lope to a trot, then walk and do a little side-pass. It gets the horse thinking and into a rhythm.

Next I would walk the horse along, then raise my hand a little, tightening it slightly at the same time. The horse should feel that. If she doesn't stop, I would count to three, then pick up one rein at a time, slow and easy, alternating sides (this is especially important on a horse wearing a snaffle).

The broken snaffle has a clamping effect that teaches the horse to raise its head and stiffen its jaw when you pull with both hands. The horse braces for the pull by raising its head and stiffening, which dumps the horse on its front end and gives the horse a hollow back; the horse then usually goes even faster.

The key to slowing a horse in a snaffle is to squeeze and release your hand, to signal and soften instead of taking a dead hard pull. If you keep pulling straight back, the horse will continue to get worse for the rest of its life. Alternate and give, as though you had

Teaching a horse to go on a slack rein makes the horse responsible for its own balance—and results in a more elegant picture.

thread for reins. Teach the horse that there is a light contact first, and if the horse responds to that, there will be no hard, uncomfortable pull. If the horse does not respond, use more contact (there are some horses that will need a lot of work at the walk before they become light and sensitive).

> **One of the secrets of resistance-free riding lies in the rider respecting his or her horse.**

12

❀ ❀ ❀

Resistance-free Western Horsemanship and Hunt-Seat Equitation

Resistance-free riding is custom made for the Western horsemanship or hunt-seat equitation rider. These riders learn to be really aware and sensitive to the ripple effect emanating from the horse. They can tune into the cadence and steadiness that they want in their ride. In turn, they are able to really show their skills to the judge during the class. This total harmony between horse and rider is what is being judged in equitation classes, and without homing in on that ripple effect, the equitation rider ends up riding on the outside without that finished look.

In all the years that I have judged at different world shows, I cannot remember a world champion who did not use his or her eyes properly. You can spot them when they come into the ring for the class—their open eyes check out the whole ring. Their circles are exact. When they make their transitions at the markers, they are right on, and thus get maximum points. The rider that uses his or her eyes in the equitation class properly is the one who has that look of an eagle. You can see the rider's confidence glowing.

If a rider is constantly looking down, he or she is saying to the judge, "I'm not sure about this horse, but we're going to get through this." By looking down, the rider is asking the horse, "Are you going to make it, too?"

Breathing is all-important in equitation classes—the smart riders know they have to keep the gasoline in the tank. During transitions they keep breathing so that they continue to ride at their full ability throughout the entire movement. This keeps the transitions fluid. A big part of your score comes here. Scared riders hold their breath a little, while the resistance-free riders who keep on breathing flow through the classes with ease.

Preparatory commands make cues invisible for top scores. I find that those who use preparatory commands set everything up well. The good rider keeps his or her horse obedient—with the help of preparatory commands.

The mental attitude of the equitation rider also plays a big part in his or her success. The mental attitude that good riders project in the pattern is "Yes, I'm so confident." You see it in their eyes and their face. They seem so self-assured, they almost make you feel that if you don't place them, you're a dummy. It intimidates a judge a little bit. That confident attitude will make the judge look at you a little harder.

It is of utmost importance to select an equitation horse whose attitude complements your own. If you have an active, strong personality, your horse should be a little laid back and forgiving. If you are slow and patient, you can get along with a hotter horse that is more sensitive. The key is to complement, not to match.

In respect to sizes of horse and rider, it is very appealing to see a twosome who are similar in size. That's why a good pony is so appropriate for the young rider. Admittedly, it's always cute to see those little ones on top of the biggest horse in the class, but they usually don't have any leg control. In some cases their legs don't even touch their horse's sides. The horse is working mainly off the announcer.

The least attractive pairing is the towering rider dominating a small horse. You begin to wonder who should be riding whom. With these riders, there is never any question about putting leg on the horse—they can almost touch their feet together beneath the horse's belly.

A horse with flatter sides makes it easier for a rider to maintain good leg position, as does a horse with easy gaits who works well as an individual. Some horses are more comfortable in a group class, and these don't always show to advantage when it comes time to leave the line and work, or when they have to be in the ring alone.

Exercises and Practice Tips

If you are really serious about your horsemanship, you ought to spend at least three days a week doing drills and exercises, utilizing either the round pen or the longe line.

Polish your patterns by practicing on foot. This keeps your horse from learning the patterns and anticipating each maneuver, yet lets you have the security of knowing each step by heart. Don't forget to include your preparatory commands for each transition while you're practicing. You can put out markers at varying distances to practice adapting your circle size and overall rhythm in the maneuvers.

Practice in your mind as well, both at home and just before your classes. Keep it positive! You can also draw your patterns on paper and mentally rehearse your ride.

I like to see equitation riders work a lot at home on transitions and circles, using cones or markers to define patterns. Markers outside the ring teach the rider to do large or small circles without dropping their eyes. A good way to practice using the ripple effect when riding at home is to change the speed of your gait while maintaining the same rhythm. Do a lot of slow walks, fast walks, slow jogs, and posting trots. You should be able to keep the horse at exactly the gait and speed you want.

Breathing before going into a class—and just before doing the individual patterns—is essential. You should take at least three to five deep breaths before you set out, filling your "gas tank" to the max. In pattern work, many young people tend to stop breathing part way through the pattern. Remind yourself to keep on breathing as you proceed.

Practice preparatory commands at home. Set up cones and practice stopping and starting beside them. Strive to make your transitions as your shoulder passes the cone, beginning your preparatory commands three strides before the marker. After you have mastered this, move the preparatory commands to two strides before the marker, and then one stride. The transition should be as graceful and clean as a dance step. Remember that invisible aids are what win horsemanship classes. When you and your horse are as one, the harmony will be at its maximum.

Mentally visualize the perfect go as you work. If you have a problem, use your mental eraser and get rid of it. Don't let it hang around to bother you. Erase it and go on.

A good coach or trainer is invaluable, as you need help with developing and maintaining your resistance-free skills. It's also helpful to have friends who are in the same program, as you can have interesting discussions with them and your instructors. Having outside input can be very helpful.

> **The resistance-free rider's biggest challenge may be to find something good in every horse. Rise to that challenge, and you and your horse will win.**

CASE STUDY 4211: *Bill is seventeen and very sports-oriented. He is in his last year of showing as a youth. He is quite athletic and considers himself to be well coordinated. His problem is that whenever he stops his horse with precision at a marker in a Western horsemanship class, he almost bounces out of the saddle.*

Whenever Bill brings his horse from a lope to a walk, the horse gets strong and on the muscle. Instead of walking, the horse jigs. It is very frustrating for Bill because the harder he tries, the worse it gets.

The first thing Bill has to remember is that riding is an art form and not a sport where being fast or strong counts for much. The harder you try and the more physical effort you blast forth can really take the finesse out of your riding.

Bill should check the angle and tightness of his knees when he stops. Many times very athletic riders will grip tightly with their knees, which also tightens the seat, taking their center of gravity up off the horse.

To solve this problem, the rider needs to let the knees and seat relax around the horse's barrel.

Visualize how hot candle wax drips down and around the

candle when it melts. Your legs and seat should have that same effect when stopping your horse.

And most important, remember, less is more. Don't try to power your way out of a situation. First, try doing less.

Resistance-free riders hold themselves responsible for a higher standard than anyone else expects of them. Never make excuses for yourself.

13

❀ ❀ ❀

Resistance-free Reining

The ringwise reiner who uses resistance-free riding will get maximum points out of each movement. The ripple effect and cadence achieved in the slow and fast circles give reiners an exactness and a perfection in communication with their horse.

Eyes are important to the reiner. You must know where you are in the ring and how far you are from the wall. Your circles will look like watermelons instead of oranges if you haven't got good visual judgment. You'll stop short of your markers on rundowns, losing points each time. That alone can push you out of the top ten easily. Eyes are so important. I can't emphasize that enough.

If a rider isn't breathing effectively, you'll see a tightness in his or her back and a bounce in the stop. The rider will get quick in his or her preparatory commands. A reiner who doesn't breathe in the ring will scare the horse a little on the way from the warm-up ring to the show ring. If you are nervous, you must force yourself

This is an example of what we call breaking at the loin. Notice how softly this horse uses itself and gets into the ground.

to take deep breaths, especially when you start the pattern. Then just let practice take over.

Preparatory commands for the reiner are a must. A reiner who gets in a hurry loses form, and loses points, while the reiner who uses preparatory commands can build to a crescendo as he or she performs each movement. By practicing turnarounds and other movements at home, the reiner can perfect his or her preparatory commands in slow motion, then add speed later for maximum scores.

A reiner always has to keep thinking. Off pattern means a goose egg, and it's very discouraging to have that happen after you've paid your entry fees and worked so hard. It's not really fair to your horse, either. Pilot error isn't the horse's fault.

Your mental confidence relays right into the horse. The best riders mentally feel everything flow perfectly and are looking for every movement to be better than the last. The rider who has this confidence has an advantage over the rest of the class.

Hands are important for all resistance-free riders, but especially so for the reiner. They are essential in producing the spectacular runs that it takes to win in today's shows; they are also important in making sure that your horse stays fresh and enjoys a long and healthy career.

The rider who panics and grabs a horse too quickly while competing is in for a ride that will just get worse and worse. Once you have lost the lightness created through the slack rein, your horse becomes heavier and duller. This takes away your chances for the crisp, blazing runs that earn maximum scores.

Most reining horses sour and burn out early in their careers because their riders push them too roughly and yank on their

The reiner who leaves out preparatory commands and substitutes strength for finesse will have results like this one.

mouths. When this occurs during a stop, a turn, or even a circle, the horse gets scared of being hurt during that particular movement.

These horses are easy to spot. They are stiff, scotching, or locking up during their patterns. You can feel this beginning to happen right through your hands. As you begin to take a contact with your horse's mouth, you should feel the horse yield and give just from the taking up of the slack. If you begin to feel the opposite, if the horse begins to pull back or checks in its movement, that is a trouble sign. You may notice that the horse raises its head or gets stiff in its shoulders and neck. Only slow, confident hands that use preparatory commands will help teach the horse to once again trust its rider.

The right horse for an amateur reiner is not necessarily the right horse for the experienced rider who seeks a championship prospect. The novice needs a horse with plenty of mileage who is able to teach a beginner the sport without falling apart.

Trainers look for reining prospects by examining their breeding and athletic ability (certain bloodlines do seem to enjoy consistent success in reining and in cattle events). These young prospects then are developed under a training and riding schedule that includes a lot of slow basics. It's easy to put the spark in a horse who has its foundation firmly in place, and it won't take very long to then bring the horse to a performance peak.

Exercises and Practice Tips

The best way to learn to perform reining maneuvers is from a good, honest horse. An old practice horse is often the best trainer and teacher.

To practice circles, I like to place a pole in the center of the arena and attach a swivel ring to it. Then I tie a twenty-foot rope to the ring; the swivel allows it to turn freely. I ask my riders to pick up the end of the rope, which is knotted, and practice circling. If they deviate too much in the circle size, the pole will move. If they cut in, the rope will drag.

Most people see reining as a high-powered event that is won by power riding; but it's really the rider with finesse who wins. Just because you see someone slide sixty feet, that doesn't mean you have to slide seventy-five. Reining patterns should be ridden with the mental attitude of a figure skater, not with the idea to run the hardest, slide the fastest, and turn the quickest. Reining is an art form with style and feel.

To improve the use of your hands and legs, practice counterlead work, counting the strides before your change (it is good to vary the number of strides between changes). I like to have riders count strides out loud, looking to the left or right instead of down at the horse. This way the hands and the legs have to take over.

To improve the use of your seat, do a lot of body tightening and loosening at the walk and jog. Make a fast circle, then a slow circle. Feel your energy peak, then relax. You want to have your horse respond to this action in your body. I recommend doing repetitions of eight two or three times a week.

Develop the ripple effect by long-trotting your horse and driving the horse into its stops with your seat. Gallop big and small circles, using your body weight to increase and then decrease the horse's rhythm and speed. Do not use the reins. This work can also be done at the walk.

A reiner's eyes should always be focusing on the next movement, whether it be the second circle or the rundown. At home, practice looking to the horizon.

Practice breathing exercises one to three times a week, depending on your level of relaxation. You want to be able to breathe in time with your horse's gaits. The stronger you want your horse to be, the deeper you breathe. The softer you want your horse, the softer you breathe.

Use preparatory commands generously at the walk before stopping, teaching the horse to tune into you. Soften your back and sink into your seat bones. Visualize sitting in a swing and pumping to go higher. Exaggerate these preparatory commands for turn-arounds, as this creates a pureness in your horse's form and position. Establish consistent use of preparatory commands until they come as naturally as good breathing.

You can never mentally practice the perfect run enough. Your internal video should be going full tilt. Reiners can learn to carry that perfect run in their mind so well that they can even hear the judge scoring them (good scores, of course).

Don't school a horse on patterns. Practice them in your mind or on a piece of paper. If you practice your patterns in training, the horse will anticipate the patterns and cheat on you. Never put two movements together unless you're actually in competition. For

Good turnarounds are a product of resistance-free riding. This horse is arched properly and ready to get the job done.

example, don't school lead changes by doing figure eights. Instead, do several circles with an occasional lead change to a new circle. That way the horse does not anticipate a lead change every time the horse comes to the center of the ring.

Schooling shows are a great place to tune up a horse; they also give you the added advantage of being able to use two hands on the reins to keep the horse honest. You can break up the standard routine a little and keep the horse fresh, using both hands in order to position the horse precisely.

It's a good idea to become an expert on the type of ground and outside attractions to be found at each show facility. A journal works well for logging in notes on whether the footing is sandy, sticky, or first-rate, and whether there is a good warm-up area. Walk your ring and find all the good spots. It's also helpful to note down whether there are rattly portable grandstands, permanent wooden stands, or a nice viewing area where you can get out of the weather for a while and relax. Sometimes a young horse is upset by a lot of noise from the grandstands, particularly children leaping from bench to bench.

Be aware of the location of the out gate and the warm-up pens. These distractions may affect your horse's performance.

Don't win the class in the warm-up ring. Always save just a little for the show ring. If you never push a horse to its limits, the horse is much more likely to keep trying, particularly during the warm-up. The horse will also last a lot longer. After all, winning the class in the warm-up ring doesn't buy your gas for the trip home.

Set goals for your riding for each week, each month, for six months, and for the year. You also should plan what you want to see three, five, and ten years down the road. Keeping a journal can be useful in logging in your progress. A good instructor or ground person is essential for helping you maintain steady improvement.

> **A resistance-free rider never confuses his or her horse with what it does not know.**

CASE STUDY 8752: *Melissa is a schoolteacher and has a top reining horse. He's thirteen years old and has been successful for years. She bought him about a year ago, and at the beginning of the year, she was winning everything. Now he's starting to cheat, getting bouncy on his stops and fading on his rundowns, quitting before the marker.*

We know the horse isn't the problem because he did work well before. Melissa has to be doing something wrong. If this horse were three and suddenly started popping his nose, I'd suspect that he had way too much bridle on him. However, this horse has a lot of mileage and has probably been in several different bits. I think our problem is the rider.

Melissa should do a lot of loping and stopping, learning to really use her upper body. I suggest that she work back and forth in the middle of the ring. About three strides from the fence, she should sit back and down a little, keeping her lower back soft and letting her legs go slightly forward. This warns the horse that a stop is coming. She should then take an even hold on both reins to ask the horse to stop at the fence. She doesn't have to pull on him at all because the fence stops him. This exercise is called "fencing" a reining horse.

Her preparatory commands will include a settling of the upper body at about three to four strides out from the fence; her eyes and chin should be up, and she cannot pull back on the reins. She has to learn to prepare the horse for the stop so that he doesn't worry about getting jerked in the mouth.

With practice, the horse will learn that Melissa isn't going to ask him to stop until she makes that body movement. The horse will start getting his hocks back underneath him and working again without resistance. He won't get those big pulls any more, so he will be a much happier horse.

**Resistance-free riders with confidence in themselves
inspire confidence in their horses.**

14

❀ ❀ ❀

Resistance-free Cutting

The cutter who knows resistance-free techniques will get the best goes. However, there is one paramount reason for the cutter to use these techniques: whenever a rider resists the movement of the horse, he or she risks pulling the cow right out of the horse. Any time you aren't resistance-free and the horse starts to think about you instead of the cow, the horse is going to lose the cow.

A cutter who goes with the flow and maximizes the ripple effect will get a lot out of his or her horse. There is a certain rhythm to the perfect cutting ride. The ripple effect lets a rider really gather the energy from the horse to make those crack turns.

The cutter who doesn't use his or her eyes can ruin a ride. All you have to do is look down once, and you won't see what happens if the cow makes a move or starts to lift its head. You can't read your cattle if you lose eye contact. Poor use of your eyes will come back and bite you every time.

You can take the cow right out of your cutting horse if you don't ride it to the best of your ability. Cutting requires the optimum harmony of horse and rider.

Even just walking into the herd, you've got to check them over. You might see one with a bad eye—you probably won't want it. Another might be a little crippled. Being able to see and read the cattle is important in determining what kind of character a cow might have.

You want to go into the herd with your eyes in a sponge mode to absorb everything. You want to be able to use both sides of your pen as you get your cow set up out front. Keeping that cow in the middle is what wins classes.

If a cutter looks down or watches the ground or the horse's ears, he or she will get in trouble on one side or the other. Looking past or through that cow while reading it can really improve your ability to handle it.

Starting and stopping is where preparatory commands are most important for the cutter. The cutter goes into the herd and lifts the reins slightly when selecting the cow. Once the cow clears the herd, the horse is on its own. During the two and a half minutes that follow the start, you're going to want to let the horse do his thing and follow the horse's motion. The cutter will use a little preparatory command if the horse becomes what is called "leaky." That means that after the cut is made, the horse slowly pushes the cow too far out of the herd. The aware rider will use his or her seat bones and upper body to warn the horse that it's losing position.

The cutter who enters the pen with a positive attitude, looking for the best cattle, is going to get the most out of his or her horse. The rider who goes in there upset about losing a cow or a back fence last time is going to be adversely affected. You've got to take advantage of every possible edge. Positive thinking is one of the best edges when all other things are equal.

The resistance-free cutting-horse rider breathes properly at all times. Before you enter the pen, warm up your horse slowly and thoroughly, long-trotting and loping circles. The lope or gallop is a good gait for your warm-up because it encourages rhythmical breathing for both horse and rider. When you are called in to work, take a few seconds to breathe an extra-deep breath to ensure relaxation.

As the work starts and you make your selection, it is very easy to hold your breath. This is especially true if the cow you select is a little rank. It happens to the best. If you feel your legs start to get tense, that should be a red light to alert you to keep breathing. You should also take three or four deep breaths between cattle. After you have established this as a habit, you will find that your works will start to smooth out.

Position is critical for the resistance-free cutter. When you need to score points on both sides of the pen, it is important to use both sides of your body. In addition, the cutter who stays soft in his or her back will be able to absorb the tremendous energy and drive generated by the horse.

A lot of cutters brace themselves with their feet out in front of their body. That's just a cheap way of hanging on. The rider who stays balanced and moving with the horse never chances getting behind or in front of the horse's movement. Either of these mistakes can cause a real avalanche of problems that results in losing a cow.

Breeding really tells when it comes to picking a cutting prospect. The price of futurity prospects in the sales has really skyrocketed. The well-bred colts always sell for a big price. They are athletic and show a lot of cow. This is easy to spot if you can see them in front of a cow.

The term "cow" refers to the horse's instinct to work or handle a moving animal; it is not limited to cattle. This response to movement is automatic in even a young horse, with only a small introduction to what is wanted. Some horses show instincts that are better suited to reining; others demonstrate cutting moves early on.

One reason quarter horses are popular as polo mounts is that they have this instinctive response to movement, whether it be a calf or a ball. It is important not to stifle that attentive focus on movement.

Exercises and Training Tips

A high-quality training program is essential for the cutter. Even though you are only working for two and a half minutes, you have to be physically at your peak. For every minute of work in the pen, you should figure in a half hour of galloping at home every other day.

Notice the total focus and harmony of Bobby Ingersoll on Kiger Cougar, a three-year-old Mustang stallion owned by Kiger Cougar Foundation at the Reno snaffle bit futurity during the cutting phase.

Time in the round pen will help you develop a strong seat. Have a ground person reverse you at the gallop while you ride with no hands and no bridle on the horse. You'll eat a little dirt at first, but you'll really learn to sit deep. A good instructor or ground man is indispensable to keep you on the right track and improve your performance.

A great exercise for learning to read cattle and get fit at the same time is to work cattle on foot. Walk into the herd, pick a cow, and take that cow to the other end of the arena. After you get out of position and lose the cow a few times, you'll start to be able to anticipate the cow's movements (especially after the cow's gotten away a few times and made you run all the way from the top of the arena to the other end).

Working cattle on foot really teaches you to move quickly in order to stay on top of the action. I know a lot of old cowboys will laugh, but believe me, this is one of the quickest and best ways to learn to handle and read cattle.

Spend as much time as you can in feedlots and on ranches handling cattle. Even just sitting and watching will give you some insight into how a cow thinks. Granted, cattle are not deep thinkers, but neither are some people.

Watch champion cutters on video and analyze their moves. Use the slow-motion button to break down each maneuver into its key elements. Look at specific parts of the rider each time through and see how they fit into the entire picture. Don't waste time watching the mistakes that are made.

At the show, you have to know where the back fences are, and you need to establish a mental harmony with your turnback people. You've also got to be reading your cattle from the moment you pull into the show grounds. Be sure to also study the cattle during other riders' goes.

In the warm-up ring, work on breathing during long-trotting and galloping. Practice breathing every two strides, then every three. Another good exercise to relax your breathing and improve your rhythm and timing is done at the long trot. Stand up in the stirrups and inhale for four strides, sit and exhale for four strides, stand and inhale for four strides, and so forth. Do this exercise for several minutes until you feel relaxed.

For cutters, failing to plan is planning to fail. Well ahead of time (not at the last minute) you should have your selection made, and you ought to communicate to the turnback people and herd holders what your horse can do. They need more instructions than just, "Hey you, stand there."

Cutters want to end with a crescendo. If you can build confidence in yourself and your horse as you work you will finish strong. Start with a soft cow, and keep in mind that you aren't going to take home the big paycheck with a vanilla go. Remember that a sanitary (clean) run is what takes home the paychecks.

The resistance-free rider knows that two and a half minutes of success pays for years of failure.

CASE STUDY 8651: *Mark is forty years old and thinks he's in really great shape. He runs about four miles a day. For fun, he rides cutters. Whenever his horse makes a really hard turn, however, he overrides and gets behind the horse. This distracts and disrupts the horse, and he loses the cow.*

Mark tries to muscle himself around on the horse. He actually brings himself up off the horse's back and raises his center of gravity, making it easy for the horse to move right out from under him. By the end of the run, the two of them are really out of synch, and it's a relief to hear the whistle.

Men especially have a tendency to solve difficulties by using strength, while women are more likely to first try finesse. Cutting is one of those situations where using too much strength just makes the problem worse.

Mark has to sit deep during those drives and turns and keep his equilibrium as low as possible, and he'll find that the horse improves and stays locked into the cow. Staying well centered will stabilize his center of gravity and allow him to work in harmony with his horse.

Your awareness must stem from your center, just above your pelvis, and not from your head. It's easy to think of riding in terms of positioning your head and working down, but that will not fix anything for more than a few moments. In contrast, starting from your center gives you incredible stability that makes it much easier to achieve correct position.

A great exercise to improve stability is to ride in the round corral at a lope with your hands on top of your head, locked together, while someone reverses the horse at random. This can work wonders.

Resistance-free riders know there is never a wrong time to do the right thing.

15

❀ ❀ ❀

Resistance-free Team Penning

In team penning, the principles of resistance-free horsemanship still hold true. In penning, the name of the game is best time, but you must be able to keep control of your horse and of the cattle you select. By using your eyes properly, you can view the entire herd while cutting out one animal. You can get quieter moves this way without stirring the cattle. You will also be less likely to override your turns and waste time.

You need to watch for cows with the correct number that are easy to get and appear easy to handle. Use your eyes to be aware of every inch of the pen, no matter how fast you are going, and know what cattle are in front of you as well as behind. Know which cattle are going to cross over the line. Penning the wrong animals or letting stock with the wrong numbers over the line results in major faults. You can't be looking down at your horse.

Breathing properly will keep both you and the horse relaxed

There is nothing like penning your cattle in good time to make your day.

and able to concentrate to your fullest. A lot of novice penners tend to hold their breath for the first minute and a half, and consequently aren't working up to par during that time. Their movements get quicker and quicker as they go along, and by the end of their run, everything is a jammed mess. Remember what the old cowboys say: you can pull a rope but you can't push it. Pushing cattle too hard and fast makes them wild, and that costs you time.

Preparatory commands enable your horse to maneuver on his own after your cues. They keep the cow in the horse and let the horse move a little faster—perhaps a tenth of a second, and that can make the difference between a paycheck and nothing.

In team penning, your mental attitude can easily deteriorate into one of panic; this is common in all speed-oriented competitions. You must know how to get yourself out of the panic mode and back into a thinking mode. Force yourself to breathe—and to look up at the horizon. Just knowing how to correct the problem will often prevent the problem from ever arising.

Without understanding the ripple effect, the team penner loses the timing necessary for balanced turns and optimum stops. If the rider just pulls and turns, it wads the horse up and doesn't let it turn efficiently. I've seen a lot of team penning lost with a locked-up turn or an out-of-control stop.

Watch the world champion teams perform on video. They make it look ever so easy. No fuss, no muss, just well-executed maneuvers and no wasted effort.

Exercises and Riding Tips

Team penning is an offensive sport, where you and your teammates take the initiative and work the herd, as opposed to the defensive sport of cutting, where the goal is trying to keep the cow out of the herd. There are a number of exercises and tips that can help the resistance-free team penner make his or her gather in good time.

Start by selecting the best-broke horse you can find. Horses who have been trained for cutting and reining are perfect. For novices, an old, well-broke horse is a lot more forgiving than a young horse.

Find the right partners as well—partners who are athletically and mentally compatible. This is a team sport. Keep your expectations realistic, however, and forgive each other for mistakes. Don't get mad at your partners; the next mistake may be yours. After all, justice sometimes is served. I remember three women whose husbands thought not good enough to partner them; the three women rode together and won the event.

When practicing at home, do a lot of half turns on the wall. These help improve your harmony and confidence for turns in the open. Trot down the wall and stop square and straight. Stand for a moment. Then slowly take a feel of your horse's mouth with a direct rein, following with an indirect rein that turns the horse's front end toward the wall. As soon as your horse begins the turn, use outside leg pressure and inside leg support in coordination with your hands. When hands and legs are in harmony, the horse will roll over its inside hock with a crack. Work this drill in both directions until it is equally easy either way.

Don't overdo it—in practice or while performing. If you override and overcue, you will be guaranteeing that your horse and the cattle will be even harder to handle because all of them will be stirred up like a tornado in Kansas.

Work on your position at home; you can't be thinking about it during your ride. It is very easy to get sloppy and brace yourself with your legs instead of sitting up and riding correctly. Don't just park your feet on the dashboard; that slows down your horse and puts you half a beat behind the action.

When you arrive at the show, sit down with your partners and plan your strategy on paper. Find out how many teams there are, how much time you'll have, and figure out when you'll be up. Go out in the pen and watch your cattle. Be able to identify them. Know which ones are sticky, which ones are runners, who's buddied up with whom, and who is hardheaded. Then plan your warm-up. By practicing at home, you should know what works to get your horse ready.

Many riders try galloping circles, long-trotting, and breathing in rhythm while looking left and right; all are good preparation exercises—both at home and in the warm-up ring. You can also try exercises that slow your hands down. Simple hand yields are very good; you want to lift the horse's shoulders to prepare the horse for the possibility of overriding cattle. Keep the horse soft as you stay soft. Many riders get rough with their hands in timed events and contribute to making their horses hot. Keep your legs and back soft as well. Jamming your horse around in the warm-up area is certainly no way to prepare. Bend over and work on softening your back so that you are flexible and supple for the class. This really develops your ability to move with the horse and absorb its movement.

This sport is a team effort. One person rarely wins the class. Share responsibilities with your teammates, and share the glory as well. Learn to get along and communicate. You are completely dependent on one another, after all.

How a rider handles success is not as important as how he or she handles failures.

16

❅ ❅ ❅

Resistance-free Hunters and Jumpers

The hunter-jumper rider who uses resistance-free riding techniques can become a superstar. Whether you're facing two-foot verticals in hunter hack, or five-foot oxers in a jumper class, you can use resistance-free riding to give yourself a safer and better trip around the course.

Striding becomes easier when you feel the ripple of the horse's movement to its fullest. If you are fully aware of the ripple and flow of the horse's gallop, you can cruise around the course as though you were a centaur. It will become no more difficult to meet the fences in stride than it is for you yourself to step over a curb.

Your eyes will be able to judge the entire course as a whole, always looking on to the next fence. One of the most common mistakes riders make is to stare at the jump itself. Riders tend to end up where they look, and if you're staring at the ground, you may soon get there. This is especially true when jumping natural obstacles, such as ditches.

Instead, as you arrive at each obstacle, look ahead to the next. Let your open eyes keep you oriented in the arena.

You must not cut the corners in hunter and hunt-seat equitation classes over fences because that can cause the horse to drop a hind lead or get a poor line into the next fence. For the jumper rider, cutting corners too tightly, especially in the first round, can result in dropping rails.

As the combinations and lines get tougher, good breathing keeps you relaxed and confident in the horse. You must remember to continue breathing because nervous riders have a tendency to hold their breath from start to finish, and that can result in tension as well as bad judgement. As your horse approaches the fence, use preparatory commands to help keep the horse soft. Collect the horse with your upper body, shifting your weight back and lifting your shoulders. A soft horse is able to round its back and use itself over each fence.

Be confident that you will do well on the course, and feel good about the trip. You can't let past performances or certain "bogey" fences bother you. If your horse senses you are nervous about a particular fence, the horse may rush it or refuse it.

The resistance-free hunter-jumper rider will not interfere with his or her horse over fences, allowing the horse to perform at its best and safest. The average hunter has a very good idea of how to get over a jump if you leave the horse alone.

The very best horse to teach you how to jump is a well-mannered school horse who doesn't refuse, and who takes good care of its rider. More advanced riders will be able to use the ripple effect and preparatory commands to change and improve the performance of more difficult horses. You can only reach this stage, however, if you start with a horse who will take care of you.

Parents, don't overmount your kids. It doesn't do any good to buy a beginner the fanciest horse in the barn if that horse won't be a babysitter. Nor does it do any good to put that kid on a piece of junk that won't jump. The first horse will result in a ruined horse and a scared rider; the latter horse will result in a scared, frustrated rider and a horse that is still worthless.

You'd be surprised just what you see in some classes over fences. One mother sent her young daughter into a horse-show class over low fences, stood and watched at the gate while the horse refused three times and was eliminated without jumping a single jump, and then said loudly to the child, who was in tears, "I knew he wouldn't do it."

So why did they enter the class?

There is always a certain amount of difficulty when you start showing over fences, and sometimes it takes a few classes before you finally get around an entire course reasonably well, but you don't need to undermine yourself before you even start by using the wrong horse. Find Mr. Right. It doesn't matter if he is ugly or handsome, chestnut or purple, 14.1 or 17.2. You can even put up with a horse who isn't especially sound if the horse is steady and dependable. Granted, it's better to have a perfectly sound horse, but you will probably soon graduate from your first horse, so it's not important that the horse be able to take you to the Olympics.

The perfect beginner's horse is often someone else's cast-off who is ready to drop back to a lesser level and teach instead of heading for the National Horse Show. Age is not a drawback. Many faithful lesson horses teach well into their twenties. As long as you keep these old horses going on a daily basis, they'll last almost forever. If you ride only one day a week, however, they tend to have physical problems and eventually slow down.

Exercising and Training Tips

Safety is extremely important in all types of jumping because you can so easily get hurt. When jumping, you should always wear a helmet with a fastened chin strap. You may also want to wear a "flak jacket" cross-country, or schooling over large fences. These jackets protect your ribs and body from impact.

You also want to avoid putting too much wear and tear on your horse's legs by overjumping the horse. An excellent way to practice without jumping is to work over poles on the ground instead of raised obstacles. This gives you all kinds of practice approaching and negotiating an infinite number of courses without hurting the horse. You can set poles in cavalletti patterns, or in a simulated course. Ride deeply into your corners and set the horse up for each pole as if it were an obstacle. Strive to ride smoothly to each pole, and don't worry about whether the horse actually gets off the ground for each pole. It's more important that the horse meet the pole in stride and depart smoothly. Remember to look forward, not at the poles.

Practice distance problems with poles as well, setting varied spacings and working to either add a stride or leave out a stride at both the canter and at the trot. Make these adjustments smoothly, as you would do them in the show ring; don't "cowboy" down to a pretend fence and try to leave out your last stride by leaping from twenty feet away. Instead, increase every stride in your approach by one or two feet and cover up that distance smoothly. Do not take four normal strides and one monster step.

If you aren't comfortable with the size of the fences you are jumping, or with the way your horse is jumping them, do something about it. You may need a new instructor to help you solidify your basics. You may need to go back to jumping crossrails and cavalletti. Don't be ashamed of that.

You also may need a different horse. Not every horse is suited to jumping, nor is every jumper suited to every rider. It is far better to have a quiet horse that you have to push a little than to have a rocket that you can't control.

Ride without stirrups as much as possible. The world's best leg-maker is posting without stirrups. Work at it religiously, and you'll be one of those riders who grins long and wide when the judge calls for riders to drop their irons at posting trot. Yes, be happy! That absolutely guarantees you your chance to shine! As you become more skilled, work without stirrups as well over cavalletti and fences. You will develop a solid, secure seat.

Even if you show your horse in a pelham or kimberwick, try to practice a lot in a snaffle bit. This enables you to have a direct feel from your fingers to the horse's mouth. Because the snaffle works on the corners of the horse's mouth, rather than through a leverage effect, the horse will move more freely than when in a pelham or kimberwick.

Good riding is good riding. The tack is just decoration. Take dressage lessons, even if you never intend to compete in that sport, because it gives you a terrific foundation for any sort of riding. A good dressage rider can easily ride a Western-trained horse because he has the basic tools. It isn't always as easy for the cowboy to do the same with the dressage horse.

If you are seriously interested in jumping, spend as much time as possible riding out with a friend and jumping natural obstacles cross-country. Go over logs, ditches, banks, and whatever else you can find to jump. The more time you spend on horseback negotiating rough terrain, the better your timing will be. The simple jumps in the ring will lose their power to intimidate you. Just remember that you have to ride with finesse outdoors just as you do in the show ring. You will not do your horse or yourself any good if you spend all your time riding lickety-split over obstacles; your horse will think that there is no other way to jump.

Videotaping your practices and your show rounds can be extremely helpful in improving your jumping. Often it is difficult to feel what is happening; a videotape clearly shows a rider how he or she is doing.

Positive thinking and mental imagery is extremely important to the rider who is showing over fences. You can jump six million fences correctly every night in your mind and enjoy a better ride when you get on your horse. Don't think about crashing, think of how it feels to soar and land like a feather, and how it feels to pick up that blue ribbon when you finish. Envision an entire class from start to finish, beginning with a correct and smooth circle, eight correct jumps, and a soft transition to the walk at the end.

> **The more the resistance-free rider knows about all the riding disciplines, the less he or she will fear, and the more confidence he or she will have.**

CASE STUDY 7341: *Olga has her horse boarded with a trainer and rides once a week. She rides only English and is reasonably proficient on the flat. She runs into difficulty in hunter hack (a popular class at breed shows), where her horse often puts in an extra stride between the jumps, lands on the wrong lead for the turn, and then drops his hind lead as he comes around the end of the ring and prepares to hand gallop.*

Olga also has another major problem: she is noticeably overweight.

This is a complex problem. Olga's horse isn't moving up properly into the right length of stride because she isn't putting enough leg on him. Heavyset riders often have difficulty applying leg aids because their leg shape is more rounded, giving them less stable surface for cuing the horse.

One of the most basic changes Olga is going to have to make in order to be really competitive is to lose weight. It's really hard to present your horse at its best when you are heavy. When you are a big person, it's easy for you to disrupt your horse's balance by shifting your weight one way or the other.

The athletic demands of classes like hunter hack are also easier

Hunter hack is a class requiring finesse as well as skill. Your balance affects your horse with every step.

to meet when you are in better shape. At the very least, Olga needs to ride much more often and sharpen her reflexes so that she can control her horse's striding.

Work over poles on the ground will help her master the lengthening and shortening of stride so that she can get her distances right. She should also practice moving into and out of a hand gallop until she can make the transition in a smooth, positive fashion, without a struggle. As she lands from that last jump and prepares to go around the corner, she needs to hold her inside hand a little higher and the outside leg held against her horse's side so that the horse lands on the correct lead.

When old horses are retired or die, a library is lost.

17

❀ ❀ ❀

Resistance-free Trail Class

Western trail class is one of the most subtle yet intense classes you can find. It demands a rider-horse combination that is both patient and brave. The unusual obstacles found in stake classes can intimidate a horse who doesn't have full confidence in its rider.

Resistance-free techniques are very useful in trotting a serpentine and working through obstacles that require tight maneuvering. If you have mastered the ripple effect, you will be better able to negotiate the walk-over or lope-over. When the horse steps over the obstacle with its left leg, you put your weight in the right stirrup to get the horse to lift its leg higher and land between the two poles.

In the lope-over obstacle, your timing and cadence must be perfect. The horse is expected to land and jump in the same instant; the spacing is tight, at six and a half to seven foot spacing, giving the horse little room for error. The ripple effect can help you get a top performance.

The trail-horse rider must maintain a constant awareness of his or her horse's position in the obstacles.

You must feel the energy come up squarely through the seat of your pants to get your horse moving squarely and directly. If the horse isn't positioned properly before approaching the obstacles at any gait, the horse is going to tick or knock down the obstacles from a lack of confidence, or put in extra steps.

At any gait you must use your eyes to maximum effect. As you go over walk-overs, trot-overs, and lope-overs, you can't look down at the poles or the horse will hit them.

You must be able to navigate the backthrough keeping the horse centered and away from both poles. Visualize yourself following the center line of a highway. This is especially important if the backthrough is elevated. In backing through barrels, open eyes give you a good sense of where you are and when you are about to tick the barrel. Remember, in tough competition, a tick can be the difference between first and last.

Preparatory commands—lifting the slack out of the reins and sitting more deeply in the saddle—can help keep horses soft and relaxed through any sort of backthrough obstacle. The horse needs to have confidence in you, the rider, as any distraction or distrust can result in the horse's touching or knocking down obstacle elements.

In side-passes over poles, the pole must be behind and under your heel. Narrow eyes can mislead you about the position of the pole. Riders often want to place the pole nearly under the horse's forefeet, but it needs to be back below the rider's heel. With open eyes you can glance out of the corner of your eye to see the position of the pole.

Your back must be really supple as you open and close the gate. As you approach the gate, use preparatory commands to tell your horse to wait: relax your body, settling into the saddle and letting the air out of your lungs. Keep your body centered as you reach out to work the latch; you do not want your horse to overreact

Use preparatory commands to keep your horse calm yet attentive when working obstacles.

Surprising your horse with a cue can result in a moment like this one, in which the horse responds with resistance instead of cooperation.

as you move the horse to open the gate. The opening should not be excessively large, or "the cows will get out."

You should negotiate gates smoothly and promptly, but without careless speed. Horses often anticipate the familiar moves of a gate opening, and may need practice at home, standing and waiting for several minutes between each move. Your preparatory commands will help keep your horse honest. Don't let the horse get in the habit of going through the gate routine on the horse's own. Some course designers design different gate maneuvers, and it can be tough to try and convince a horse to do it your way.

Preparatory commands before the lope can make the lope smooth, soft, and powerful. You position the horse's hip with your outside leg, hold the horse's shoulder up by keeping your inside leg at the cinch, and gather the reins for a moment of collection and give. Lope strike-offs are probably some of the most anticipated maneuvers for the horse, and are easily ruined as a result. Anticipation can only be corrected by schooling at home, making the horse wait for your commands before it lifts into the lope. You should be able to spell out the preparatory commands as easily as "A, B, C," and the horse should wait for "C" before it lopes.

A good mental attitude lets you look at the pattern as a whole and give your horse confidence and strength. The rhythm changes in this class can be a real challenge and require both softness and strength to get those super goes out of the horse. The best ride results when you achieve those rhythm changes so subtly that no one but you and the judge know what's happening.

For this class, you will want a horse who is quiet and patient, but aware and curious. The horse should be supple and obedient, yet willing to wait. The top trail horse is secure in character with an independent mind. The horse will often graze alone when out at pasture.

Exercises and Training Tips

Keep your riding and training varied and fresh. Practice obstacle work at least every other day, but with frequent changes so that the horse does not just work out of habit. Practice different techniques, such as performing an entire course on foot. Use a lot of elevated obstacles with good spacing to give your horse confidence. Remember that timing and rhythm between you and your horse comes from working correctly set obstacles that develop trust, not apprehension. Don't be afraid to get out your measuring tape and check spacing.

Don't set up impossible obstacles that can't be worked properly. Obstacles like this will destroy your horse's confidence.

I like to set up a training course built with railroad ties. They absolutely don't move when a horse ticks one, which teaches the horse to respect the obstacles.

Always finish your training sessions with a good obstacle, letting the horse finish satisfied and pleased. If you've had a long battle over some difficult problem, achieve some slight improvement, then quit that problem and go on to something that the horse does easily and well—then hang up your hat for the day.

When you go to a show, look at the trail diagram as soon as it is posted and set up an imitation course you can practice out in the warm-up area or by your trailer. It's a good idea to carry a few rails, a log or two, and some traffic cones in your trailer. Lots of times you can find stuff lying around the show ground, too. Set up your little practice course in an area where you are off by yourself, not in a high-traffic zone.

When you set up your practice course, make sure that you space your obstacles fairly. Don't blow your horse's calm by setting "trick obstacles" outside and then expect the horse to perform up to par in the ring.

Set some walk obstacles at both long and short distances, starting with them set at twenty inches and increasing the spacing between each successive obstacle by an inch. Use your body and weight placement in the stirrups to adjust your horse's stride. Work this set of obstacles in both directions, first short to long distances, then long to short distances.

One of my favorite warm-up exercises is to lay two poles parallel to one another, three feet apart. I then rake the center between them and draw a line directly down the middle, so the obstacle looks like a two-lane road with poles as borders. I have my students back through the two poles following the middle line. Then I have them stop, dismount, and see how their horse tracked. This exercise will quickly show you if your horse veered.

Another good warm-up exercise is to lope ten strides, stop, and side-pass two steps; lope nine strides, stop, and side-pass two steps; and so forth, all the way down to four strides of lope. That mentally attunes your horse to your leg and helps you focus on precision. You should also do as many hand yields as possible to lift your horse's shoulders and get the horse to accept your leg.

Riders also need to be attentive to their own warm-up, suppling their bodies so that they can ride to their optimum levels. Exercises like knee touches, which are right hand to left knee, then left hand to right knee, are excellent as long as you maintain your position and seat contact. Progress to toe touches. It is almost impossible to keep your seat bones in position during toe touches, but you should at least try.

Watching other riders in the class can be either beneficial or detrimental to your anxiety. If someone is really having a bad go, don't watch them. Only watch the good rides. The rest of the time, keep your back turned or go warm your horse up.

Just before you go into the ring, spend some time alone and envision yourself negotiating each obstacle cleanly for a perfect go. This will help you perform your best.

At home and at the show, it is beneficial to have a good ground person to help you analyze your approach, rhythm, and style through your obstacle work. A ground person can give you good feedback as to anything that is giving your horse trouble. You can also have this person fix knockdowns and adjust obstacles so that you don't have to break the flow of your schooling.

Remember that you must build a foundation for serious trail-class competition, not just create a horse who can do a few tricks. The trick horse will always let you down in the long run because the horse won't have the necessary basic skills to figure out new and different obstacles.

> **Noticing his or her faults encourages the resistance-free rider to keep trying to improve.**

CASE STUDY 002: *Donna enjoys riding in competitive trail. She's a housewife who inherited her horse from her daughter. She finds that her horse does really well on the obstacles—until he gets to the*

This shows how leaning too far actually tells the horse to move away from the gate instead of maintaining its position.

gate. When she tries to move up to a gate, the horse wants to move away.

It gets frustrating for both of them. The harder she tries to send that horse up to the gate, the more vigorously he sidles in the opposite direction.

The horse is well schooled, but this one failing keeps them out of the ribbons.

When Donna approaches a gate and reaches out for the latch, she doesn't keep her upper body supple in the middle of her back. Instead, she brings her arm out, her body stiffens, and she follows with the shoulder, causing her leg on that side to automatically push into the horse. The horse then obediently moves away from her leg, just as he's been taught.

Donna must remain aware of her upper body connection. She has to keep it stable and straight while practicing reaching in all directions. Her shoulders and arms must move independently of her leg.

**Accomplishing little things well is a step
toward doing big things better.**

18

❀ ❀ ❀

Resistance-free Barrel Racing

Resistance-free riding is important for the barrel racer as well as other speed event riders, because the bottom line for these riders is speed. The ripple effect gives you the feel of the horse, keeping you from overriding the horse and causing it to overshoot turns. You get softer moves and changes, quieter turns that are shorter and faster.

Every year I give a Purina-sponsored clinic at the National Finals Rodeo. I've noticed that there are only a few hundredths of a second between the champion and the tenth-place barrel racers. Every rider is able to run in a snaffle bit. You don't see the various traps that are so common at the playday level. This would have clued me in instantly (if I hadn't already known) that these were top riders, the best in the nation.

The key to being a top barrel racer is having the fastest time, period. The more gear you carry on your horse's head, the less

155

Resistance in the timed-event horse results in lost time on the clock.

speed you have. Even if the equipment doesn't weigh the horse down, it annoys and distracts the horse.

Your duty as a barrel racer is to hone your skills to a point that you can get the top speed out of your horse and still be able to stop with just a snaffle bit. If your horse isn't afraid of its mouth being hurt, the horse will be a better partner.

The ripple effect is extremely important to the barrel racer. You must feel the energy and drive from the horse's back and hindquarters and know where the horse's shoulders are at all times. Otherwise, you're going to hit barrels—or make unnecessarily wide turns. All it takes is one wide barrel, and there will be no money for the run.

Good eye control lets you look well ahead to your turning points and still keep a feel of the entire course. You should be looking ahead to the exact point at which you wish your horse to turn. If you stare directly at the barrel, your body will be aiming your horse at the barrel, not around the barrel. Since bull's-eyes aren't good in barrel racing, keep your eye on your turning spot.

You must also avoid looking down or back behind you. If the barrel falls, looking back isn't going to put it up again. Looking back will only slow you down.

To get that solid winning run, the "gas" from good breathing has to be coming into your body all the time. If you finish breathless, you'll know that you didn't ride to your optimum ability out there.

Many, many times a rider is having a perfect run and then the last barrel falls. Often this is because the rider was holding his or

Maintaining good position around the barrel is essential to avoid knockdown and still make good time.

her breath and making quicker and quicker moves, which resulted in the horse cutting the last corner. Not breathing can knock you right out of the money.

Preparatory commands help keep the horse's shoulders up, not diving into the dirt. For a right turn around a barrel, for example, you raise your right hand up about three or four strides before the barrel, keeping your right leg at the cinch. As the horse starts the turn, you put your weight in the left (outside) stirrup. These commands can help you bend the horse in the rib cage to give the horse more latitude around the barrel. The horse who can bend well in the body in a more upright position is more stable and balanced, and positioned better for speed than the horse who dives into his front end while tunneling around the barrel like a gopher. The balanced horse can use his hocks more efficiently to launch himself like an arrow from barrel to barrel.

A barrel-racing horse should be ridden into speed not beaten into speed. There is a distinction here. The horse who is beaten into running often holds back because the horse is expecting that hard jerk in the mouth at every barrel and at the end of the pattern. In contrast, the horse who trusts you to give preparatory commands before each turn will go full out, yet still set up upon your command for each barrel. The horse will stop at the end, secure and confident.

To win the big events, you have to have a super mental attitude that won't let itself be beaten. Focus on the individual runs, rather than on the last barrel you knocked down, the closeness of the year-end contenders, or the screaming audience. It's just you, the horse, and three big cans.

You have to have complete confidence in your horse. Things happen so fast in big-time barrel racing. The arena director is hustling you all the time, which increases the mental pressure. Unless you're prepared for this, the stress can throw you off just enough as you start your run, that you lose a few hundredths of a second of speed.

If you are serious about barrel racing, look for the best prospect you can find. It costs just as much to feed a slow horse as a fast one. Speed plus athletic ability are the keys to a winning speed event horse. A pretty face and a classy look don't matter in this practical division.

Soundness is all important in barrel-racing horses, because

these horses run hard week after week on all kinds of ground, spend many hours in the trailer, and have to put out their maximum effort every time they compete. There's a big difference between blasting out a barrel run and putting together a perfect rail ride when it comes to wear and tear on the horse. The basic ingredient for soundness is absolute correctness of structure, in both body and legs. If your horse is built like an athlete and constructed to do the job, that's the best insurance policy you can have.

Once you have found a good horse, be sure to keep both you and your horse in top athletic condition. Couch potatoes don't win speed events very often. If you really want to be a success in speed events, you have to be very aware of your horse's physical and mental training, as well as your own. Horses and riders who are out of condition are at a high risk for injury in this sport.

Exercises and Training Tips

There is more to preparing a speed-event horse than just running the patterns for an hour or two every day. A training practice like that is guaranteed to result in a sour, sore horse who will end up nowhere. Instead, plan a sensible conditioning program that will prepare your horse for the physical effort of competition and create the stamina that will sustain that effort.

A good exercise to practice at home is to gallop circles while keeping the horse's inside shoulder up, following the horse's rhythm with your inside hand and your seat. This will develop your lower-body control so that you can speed up and slow down your horse just with your body, not relying on your hands or legs.

To polish your horse's harmony and timing, do the following drill every ride. Stand parallel to a fence and reverse your horse by turning the horse into the fence. Use your inside rein to keep the horse's inside shoulder up, the outside rein to hold and push the horse and to develop a springing rhythm. After the turn, gallop your horse back down the fence line and stop. Look back to the inside with your eyes and repeat the exercise until it feels "greasy," four to six turns are usually sufficient, but you might need to make twelve to fifteen if you are having a problem. Your horse will soon learn to roll over its hocks.

Establish a good warm-up routine that includes more than just a few quick turns. You should plan a systematic warm-up that loosens up every muscle in your horse's body and also prepares the horse's and your minds for the run. Eighty percent of all horses who break down are the result of improper warming up and cooling down. A horse who has not been warmed up properly has tight muscles and tendons. Forcing this horse to put out a peak effort in this state may tear or strain crucial tissues. It will certainly result in a horse who is stiff and sore afterward, particularly if the horse is not cooled out slowly and carefully.

It's a good idea to warm up in a snaffle, working at the walk and trot and concentrating on slow hands and upper-body preparation. Make fast then slow circles. Let your body tighten then relax. When your horse is soft, change to the appropriate headgear for your run and finish your warm-up routine.

A good warm-up should include some long-trotting to let the horse stretch its stride out to the utmost and loosen up. You should also include circles and bending in both directions, as well as some rollbacks to get the horse tuned into you. For example, trot twenty strides then make two circles to the right; then trot twenty strides and make two circles to the left. Don't lope or gallop these drills; faster movements desensitize your hands to the horse's face and body.

One of the most important elements of a good warm-up is to get your mental focus in order. You should make note of which of the above drills enhance your concentration and best prepare you for your performance. You and your horse need to be in total harmony before you go into the ring—both mentally and physically.

That elaborate engine that serves you so well must be prepared and it must be maintained, and this includes letting the horse wind down after a run. However, there is not always room to let the horse slow down easily. Pull up your horse gradually if possible. If space is short, prepare your horse for the stop after you pass through the timers, giving the horse time to set up for the halt. Don't grab the reins and punish the horse for that good run; give the horse preparatory commands and ask for a controlled transition.

After your run, walk your horse and let the horse relax and catch its breath. Reward the horse for doing a good job.

Do not take off and leave the arena, throw the horse in the trailer, and speed home; this gives a tired, sweaty horse more discomfort to endure. The horse will quickly sour on the spot—and may also develop physical problems.

One of the best ways to improve is to work with a coach, a trainer, or a friend who will give you honest feedback. This person can offer a fresh outlook on ways to improve your runs. Your runs at the end of the season should show a steady improvement over your spring outings.

If the opposite is happening, that's a big red light. I'm not referring to one bad run, one off day, but a consistent downturn in speed. You can keep track of performance by maintaining a log or making a graph chart of your times. Consistent record keeping should only take a few minutes each day or week.

Try to think of improvement in terms of months, not days. It is so easy to get sucked into thinking that one bad day represents your entire life. Instead, strive to improve month by month, and don't let speed be the only criteria you use in your self-evaluation. If your horse is hard to rate, for example, spend more time schooling in this area and make notes that allow you to determine whether you are improving. If your horse is tough to stop after your run, try to improve that. You may need to choose only rodeos and shows that allow plenty of room for pulling up, or have you pull up inside the arena. The parking lot is not the best place for pulling up a horse who is out of control.

You should also work constantly on your resistance-free riding foundation. Remember that the ripple effect, good breathing, correct eye usage, good use of preparatory commands, and a good mental attitude are the keys to unlocking your ability to move with your horse. After all, no matter how fast your horse is, one resistant move on your part costs you a fraction of a second, and in the long run, that costs you money.

**Resistance-free riders do more than
just listen, they understand.**

CASE STUDY 8866: *Carol runs barrels on weekends. She started about two years ago. When she was small she rode bareback a lot, but she never had a chance to become a good rider. One of the problems she has with her gelding is that when he makes his second turn, he always knocks the barrel down. In fact, it seems that he never knocks the first one down, but always the second and third.*

One of the only ways to keep your horse from knocking down a barrel is to make sure you have your weight to the outside of the horse's turning arc. For example, when your horse is turning to the right, you will need to have your weight in your left stirrup. This lets your horse keep its inside shoulder up off the barrel and its hind leg driving under the horse.

Carol mentioned that she rode bareback a lot when younger. One of the bad side effects of riding bareback is the tendency to clamp with your legs and lean into your horse's turns. When Carol said that she only knocked down the second and third barrels, that gave it away. If you are going to have trouble, the second and third barrels will be where it will happen. You generally are breathing and using your eyes for the first barrel. But as the run goes to the second and third barrels, many riders revert to their old, bad riding habits.

Carol needs to keep her breathing rhythmic and her eyes to the horizon. To help with her breathing, she might try to use a little mental energy. Before her run, she should see herself as a large vacuum cleaner. As she approaches each barrel she should breathe longer and deeper, as though she were going to inhale the barrel. Otherwise, the pressure of the competition will cause her to fall back and hold her breath at each barrel, causing stiffness and tightness that will rob her of valuable seconds.

To help use her eyes correctly, Carol needs to keep looking past the barrel. She needs to focus on a visual point beyond the barrel, such as a person in the stands.

I would also have Carol practice this exercise and drill. When she is practicing her turns, she should drop her inside stirrup as she approaches each turn. This will help her to shift her weight to the outside of her arc. It will not take long before she feels secure using only the outside stirrup. To do this drill correctly, drop your left stirrup when turning to the left, and the right stirrup when turning to the right.

19

❋ ❋ ❋

Resistance-free Team Roping

The resistance-free team roper can make the sport look easy, and when the job is done well, it happens almost quicker than the eye can follow. These riders use the ripple effect to the maximum. They are in tune with the rhythm and timing of the horse, which creates an overall rhythm to the run.

To ensure a good run, resistance-free ropers stay relaxed and in focus during two critical times. The first is when they are waiting for their run. Everybody, including fellow competitors and the audience, is watching and waiting. The pressure builds to an incredible level, and this can cause a rider to take only shallow, tense breaths, or to even hold his or her breath. That tense feeling is a red-light situation. The tense roper must take in as much air as possible, breathing deeply to clear his or her head and become relaxed again. The other critical time for ropers to remain calm is

Team roping is a test of horsemanship, rhythm, rhythm, and rhythm.

when they are rating their steer. Riders often become so intent on that instant that they hold their breath. Again, they must concentrate on breathing.

Open eyes help keep everything in balance. If you're team roping, you'll be aware of your partner and his or her position.

Remember to look past your steer. This lets your body know what's coming up. Your mental computer will soak up the entire run and the arena, taking every factor into consideration. If you stare hard at the steer's horns, you'll hinder your follow-through. You'll also have problems when the steer changes direction or speed. Looking ahead with open eyes will enable you to adjust to any situation without affecting your balance or fluidity.

Use preparatory commands while waiting for your run, holding your upper body back over your seat and hips in a steady manner. The first signal your horse receives to leave the box is when you lean forward with your upper body and head.

The next time you use a preparatory command is when you turn the steer. Your upper body and shoulders turn in the direction that you want the horse to go. The rider who mixes up these commands will ruin a lot of horses.

To work at its best, your horse needs consistent, clear preparatory commands that give the horse confidence. The rider who lies to his or her horse by giving inconsistent commands will lose the trust of the horse, and eventually the horse will sour.

Exercises and Training Tips

Galloping lots of circles helps you develop your breathing and rhythm to a high level of harmony. Let your back stay supple and almost overdevelop that rhythm through your back and seat.

Practice changing speeds at the gallop, as well as going from the gallop to the trot. Gallop from one end of the ring to the other until you know how many strides it takes. As you gallop, keep your eyes on the horizon, looking at objects at the far end of the ring.

Mentally rehearse practice runs in your mind over and over, perfect each time. The final key to a winning run is the right mental attitude. Practice your winning run again in your mind several times before you walk into the box. See your loop flatten out in slow motion. See the ears of the steer flap in time with its run. See yourself double-hocking the steer.

Don't let your mind sabotage you. If the cattle are bad, remember that they're that way for everybody. If a negative thought slips into your mind, boot it out and replace it with a positive thought. Every time a negative thought enters your mind, you're setting yourself up for failure.

The resistance-free rider finds it is better to do a little well than a great deal poorly. Life's greatest gift is doing one's level best.

CASE STUDY 91280: *Bob has been roping for eight years and is very competitive. In that time he's had ten horses. Every horse eventually gets aggressive, becomes hard to handle in the box, and ends up running over the cattle.*

Bob is putting way too much pressure, both mental and physical, on his horses. He's using too much hard hand and leg, and is really just wearing his horses out. Even though team roping is an athletic event based on time, the sport has nothing to do with brute strength or physical power. Any time that your hands or your legs become too demanding and quick, you're going to have a horse who can't stand the pressure and burns out. These burned-out horses start looking for a way out.

Staying quiet in the box will go a long way toward making these horses last. To reestablish his finesse and restore rapport with the horses, Bob needs to really work on his breathing and relaxation before he walks into the box. Once in the box, he needs to focus on a quiet, steady hand, rather than a hand that jerks or restrains because of his insecurity.

When his horse leaves the box to follow the steer, Bob should work on following the horse's rhythm and movement instead of tuning into speed and becoming all-competitive. Speed will come when his timing and rhythm are right. When you gain finesse and become resistance-free, you will win more frequently.

20

❀ ❀ ❀

Riding Just
for Fun

There are many riders who never want to get into the high-pressure world of showing. These riders love horses and ride for recreation, enjoying the companionship of their horses. I really take my hat off to those people because they stay close to what horses are all about. These are the people who introduce their grandkids to horses and create a special bonding that makes a lifetime relationship. The horse is family to these people, not just a tool to use for work or show.

Some of these riders are professional people who perhaps only ride once or twice a month, but relieve their stress by going out to the barn and grooming their horse (horses are just about as good as psychiatry in some cases). Others enjoy working with young horses. Some like going for trail rides.

Just because you don't compete doesn't mean you shouldn't learn good horsemanship. Even if you aren't going to show, it pays

A trail ride can be a lot more fun if everyone is able to ride safely and comfortably.

to have good riding skills so that you can really enjoy yourself and your horse. Good horsemanship keeps you out of trouble and in good shape as well.

Resistance-free techniques can give you a lifetime of comfortable, effective riding. Some people never learn to ride correctly, and bounce all over their horses for their entire riding career. They justify this by saying, "I don't show."

If something is worth doing, it is worth doing well. As a pleasure rider, you may not require the degree of proficiency that is found in the world-class rider, but you should be safe, comfortable, and able to enjoy yourself. If you aren't in control, you aren't safe, no matter how quiet your horse is.

The United States Pony Club has the stated goal of "A Happy Child on a Happy Horse." I agree with that wholeheartedly. For me, it's "A Happy Rider on a Happy Horse." After all, you want your horse to enjoy being ridden as well. Developing a good rapport with a horse is important for the pleasure rider, as he or she often has a much closer relationship with a mount than most professionals achieve. There is no way to replace those long, long rides when it comes to really making a kinship with your horse.

The recreational rider who gets tense has the opportunity to take advantage of those same tools that competitive riders use: breathing, open eyes, the ripple effect, preparatory commands, and mental preparation. These five master keys will enable you to be relaxed and resistance-free hour after hour.

Exercises for the Recreational Rider

Are you sore when you get off your horse? Lots of times that alerts you to a problem area. If your knees are sore, or the bottoms of your feet are sore, or your back aches, those are red lights that tell you that you have a problem in those areas. A sore back often indicates a problem breathing correctly, and sore feet may tell you your weight is in the wrong spot. Sore knees are many times a sign of tension—try relaxing your leg and going with the ripple effect. Or your knee may be in the wrong position, too far forward or too far back.

Is your horse tossing its head? You might need to work on your preparatory commands. Perhaps you're using too much hand when you ride.

Is your horse getting too quick on transitions? Does the horse launch into a gallop instead of a lope when you see a long, inviting meadow? You might be using too much leg, or perhaps an unnecessary kick when a light aid would do.

If you're worn out when you get off your horse, you aren't enjoying a good relationship with your horse. Does the horse pull constantly, or get behind the bit? You might be nervously anticipating an unknown disaster and holding your breath, increasing the tension quotient without realizing it.

To stay in shape for riding, do some stretching exercises, such as the heel stretch in Chapter 2, before getting on the horse. I suggest that you also get off of your horse periodically during a ride and do some stretching. This will keep you limber.

When you start your ride, warm up at a walk, then progress to a slow trot or jog before going faster. Get both yourself and your horse warmed up, build to a peak, and then slow down to cool out and go back home. The more consistent you are in your riding and handling of the horse, the more consistent the horse's responses will be, and the more you will enjoy yourself.

On hard ground, listen to your horse's footfalls and try to determine their rhythm. Tune into that rhythm and see if you can modify it. Swinging your arm or a rope in time with the footfalls helps establish a "muscle memory" of the rhythm; by varying the rhythm of your swinging as you increase or decrease your body energy, you can adjust the horse's rhythm without making it choppy. Keep it pure.

When going up hills, look at the top of the hill, not down at the trail. When descending, look at the bottom of the hill. Use open eyes to watch for potential hazards such as gopher holes or broken glass.

On long, flat stretches, let your horse trot freely on a loose rein. This lets the horse loosen up and relax. At the same time you can do forward and backward swings and scissor exercises as described in Part One. This will help relax your upper body. Another good limbering exercise you can do on those same long trots or at the lope is to touch your horse's ears, then the top of his tail.

It's really helpful to get off your horse and walk for a few minutes on long rides. It gives your horse's back a rest, it keeps you loosened up, and it gives you a change of pace. Some horses have trouble descending hills, and may appreciate it if you dismount and walk down.

The recreational rider can turn riding into a Zen-like experience when he or she is in harmony with the horse. This is true whether you are practicing dressage in the arena or trail riding in the mountains.

Selecting a horse for pleasure riding depends on your personal preferences. Since your goal is to enjoy your horse, don't be prejudiced when it comes to picking one out. The attitude of the horse is most important; the breed and the looks don't matter. Don't let yourself get saddled with a hyper, difficult horse who won't let you have a good time.

You may be interested in the gaited horses, such as the Tennessee Walkers or the Paso Finos, who cover a lot of ground with speed but are perfectly smooth to ride. For the rider who doesn't ride a lot, a smooth horse is important. Or you may prefer an Arabian or quarter horse, particularly if you like trail riding.

Whatever type of horse you select, that horse should have perfect ground manners. The horse should load well and should travel easily with groups whether they are in the front, the middle, or the back. The horse should not get cranky with other horses.

The good recreational horse should be trail- and traffic-wise, able to cross water, ditches, and slopes without difficulty. The horse should be healthy and sound—and preferably an easy keeper.

CASE STUDY 6882: *Alice is sixty-eight years old and has been retired from a desk job for about five years. She's been riding at least twice a week on the trails in the area where she lives.*

Nothing but the best will do for her, and she has the most expensive saddle she could find for her horse. She believes firmly that her horse should be completely comfortable. Unfortunately, she can't seem to do the same for herself.

She always does some stretching exercises before and after she rides because she knows that she's not as limber as she used to be. But every time she finishes a ride she is always stiff and achy.

If you are getting older and still riding several days a week, you ought to be thankful that you are still enjoying your horse. But no matter what your age, you will become sore if you are staying tense and not moving with your horse.

The recreational trail horse should be safe around traffic and natural obstacles.

Trail riding should be fun. Choosing the right horse and right companion is important.

I would encourage Alice to use resistance-free exercises such as the scissors and windmill drills to relax and get in harmony with her horse. She will find herself feeling better when she finishes riding. She won't be subconsciously fighting the horse's movement.

I'd also have a look at that saddle. Just because it was expensive doesn't mean it puts the rider in the correct position. Most expensive saddles are deeply hand engraved. Sometimes the tooling is so deep that it chafes the rider's legs. A saddle with smooth fenders may be more comfortable for Alice.

The primary thing I'd emphasize is for a sore rider is to start working on resistance-free riding skills, particularly breathing. You'll know when you are using them to the fullest. You'll feel better after the ride instead of sore.

Bad riding is like a boomerang. About the time you think all is well, it hits you in the back of the head.

21

❀ ❀ ❀

Bridles, Bits, and Bosals

A good rider gets the most out of his or her horse by selecting the right bit. It's an important decision. In addition, horses can be worked in training devices such as bosals and side-pulls to improve their performance.

There are two main types of bits: snaffles and leverage (curb) bits. Each bit influences the horse differently, and both have a purpose in training.

A resistance-free rider is one with a full understanding of the bits that he or she uses. Just as a top basketball player is very conscious of the types of shoes he or she uses, it is important to know all about bits, how they work, how severe or mild various types may be, and what situations call for which bit. The behavior and feelings of the horse can be greatly affected by the bit. After all, a basketball player could probably manage on the court with a pair of cleated track shoes but will get a much better performance from

173

a set of cushioned basketball shoes.

The bit needs an educated hand. What makes a bit severe is the hands behind the bit. A ten-pound pull on a piano-wire twisted snaffle will create much more damage and exert more pain on the horse than the same pull on a large, smooth German ring snaffle. The most important information to know about a bit is how to yield to it with your hand.

Remember that you can often get a job done with tools that aren't necessarily right for the purpose, but to really achieve the refinement and finish work, you need the right tool. After all, you can drive a nail by hitting it with the side of a pair of pliers, but think about how tough it would be to construct an entire house that way. You would be struggling until you replaced the pliers with a carpenter's hammer. By the same token, you can train a horse to wear almost anything in its mouth and respond to some degree, even if it is with great displeasure, but you cannot put the polish on your horse's performance with a bit that is incorrectly designed or poorly-fitted.

Keep in mind that you can damage or hurt a horse with any bit if it is used improperly or thoughtlessly. In the right hands, a severe bit can be a tool to polish a diamond performance. In the wrong hands, it becomes an instrument of torture.

A horse who responds because it fears the pain of the bit will tighten its neck and stiffen its body to protect himself from the bit. If someone tells you that his or her horse doesn't like the bit, chances are that horse has never been introduced to the bit properly, nor been tried in different bits.

Snaffles

A snaffle is any kind of bit in which there is a direct line from the rider's hands to the mouthpiece. There is no leverage involved. Snaffle bits are the first bits used on horses in training. They come with a wide variety of mouthpieces and cheek styles that accomplish various purposes. Most of them have broken mouthpieces, but the mouthpiece can also be solid.

In general, snaffle bits are used with a rein in each hand. The snaffle exerts primary pressure on the lips of the horse, and a lesser amount of pressure on the tongue. If you pick up a broken or jointed snaffle, you will notice that it tends to "fold" in your hand.

Shown are various snaffle bits and their levels of severity rated from #1—the most forgiving—to #10—the most severe.

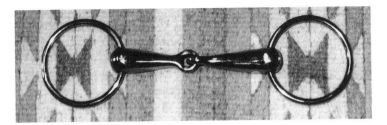

O-ring hollow-mouth (large-sized smooth tapered mouthpiece): #1

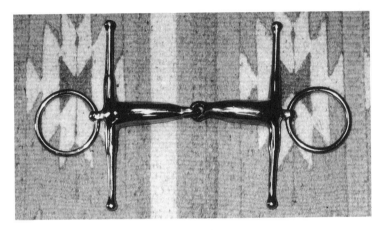

O-ring full-cheek (medium-sized smooth tapered mouthpiece): #2

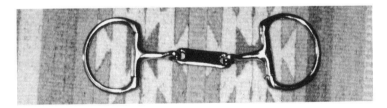

Egg-butt Dr. Bristol (medium-sized mouthpiece): #3

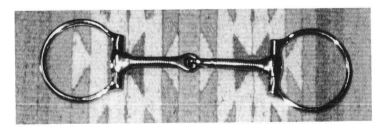

D-ring medium-sized wrapped-wire-texture mouthpiece: #5

Egg-butt (medium-sized straight-bar mouthpiece): #6

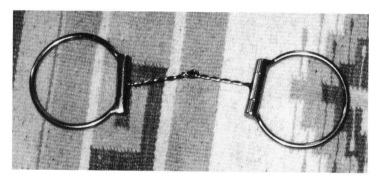

O-ring bicycle-chain (bicycle-chain mouthpiece): #9

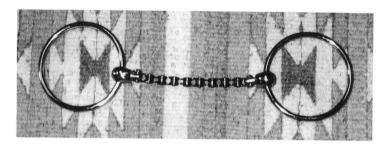

D-ring piano-wire (broken twisted-piano-wire mouthpiece: #10

It is possible to make a horse very uncomfortable with this "nut-cracker" effect. The horse will experience pressure on both sides of its jaw, and if the horse has a shallow palate, it may feel pressure on the roof of its mouth as well. The snaffle bit also puts pressure to some degree on the bars of the horse's mouth, however, the horse's tongue provides a significant amount of cushion to minimize bar contact.

An alternative to the jointed snaffle is the double-jointed snaffle. These bits are known as Dr. Bristol snaffles (with a thin, flat plate in the center, hinged on each end) and French snaffles (with a more rounded and shaped joint in the center). They conform more readily to the shape of the horse's mouth and are accepted by many problem horses, especially those with tongue problems.

There are also snaffle bits without any joints, and they can be perfectly straight (a bar snaffle, for example, like a work-horse wears) or shaped like a half-moon (a mullen-mouth snaffle). You can also find snaffles with crickets, rollers, wire wrapping, and mouthing keys. There is a bit for every purpose under the sun.

In general, the thinner the mouthpiece, the more severe the bit. Thick, rounded mouthpieces are usually the most comfortable for the horse, although some small-mouthed horses are less happy with that big mouthful and prefer the slimmer mouthpieces.

Bits are also available that are quite thin, increasing the cutting effect if used improperly. Perhaps the most severe of the thin bits is the thin snaffle bridoon bit, often seen on gaited horses in full bridles.

There are many variations of texture available in snaffles, offering progressively more severe contact to the horse. A change in texture, whether it be to a rougher, more severe surface, or simply to one with a different feel, such as a roller snaffle, can be helpful in lightening some horses, particularly those who are dull or dry-mouthed.

Some bits are very extreme, such as bicycle-chain mouth-pieces. In general, the rougher and thinner the mouthpiece, the harsher the bit. The single-twisted-wire snaffle is quite popular although it is extremely severe. Its cousin, the double-twisted-wire snaffle, is less likely to cut into the horse's tongue because there are double rows of twisted wire on each side of the center joint, instead of one.

The next mildest bit after the smooth bits would be the slow twist, a bit that can best be described as heating a square bar of steel and giving it a twist, making the edges curve around the entire bit like a barber pole.

Slightly more severe than the slow twist is a twisted snaffle that looks like a thick corkscrew. Smooth snaffles wrapped with piano wire would also be approximately as severe. The wire is closely wrapped around the mouthpiece to form a rough surface, not a cutting surface. A single piece of wire wrapped around a bit and spread apart would be very harsh.

Snaffles also differ in their style of cheekpiece. Bits with an O-ring cheek are very popular with many horses. The horse tends to pick up the bit more comfortably and handle it like an all-day sucker. Since the cheek rings rotate freely through the mouthpiece, the horse can be much lighter, as only a slight movement of the reins will cause the bit to move. Also, because the horse is picking up and holding the bit, it makes it much easier to put the horse on the bit in a correct frame. The horse is also more likely to be generating sufficient saliva to lubricate the bit and stay comfortable. The horse usually has a relaxed poll and remains relaxed in its shoulders. Its withers are able to come up, and its back is in a weight-carrying posture, not in a swayed position. Horses who are expected to work in this light, alert position, such as reining horses, are usually started in O-ring snaffles.

The D-ring snaffle is made for horses who are ridden on the bit as opposed to in the bridle. The mouthpiece is fixed to the sidepieces, which are shaped like a D. You see the bit used a lot on racehorses, as it makes them a little easier to steer. The flat surface of the D-ring keeps it from being pulled into the horse's mouth when the horse refuses to turn.

The horse can lean on a D-ring a little bit and take a firmer contact than with an O-ring. This is ideal in certain situations. A racehorse, for example, would not run well without the support of firm contact. Racehorses need that balancing influence to keep them put together. Drop the contact on a racehorse and he'll quit running (unless he's bolting). This is what makes it difficult for some riders to reschool horses off the track. The riders want to pull on the reins to stop the horse, and the horse has already been taught that pulling on the reins means to run like the wind.

D-ring bits are occasionally used on driving horses, who also go on contact. However, it is more common to see these horses in half-cheek snaffles or other types of bits. Driving etiquette is such that if you show up in a class with a bit that is out of fashion, you may not get used.

The D-ring is a more rigid bit than the O-ring snaffle because it doesn't move as freely in all of its parts. The cheeks can move outward and inward, and the center joint (if any) allows movement, but that's it. The bit has three points of movement, as compared to a full axis of movement in all directions for the O-ring snaffle. The full-cheek snaffle is most commonly seen in the hunter show ring. It has branches protruding from a smaller ring that help frame the horse between the bit cheeks and aid in steering. It is also considered to be a very pretty bit on a fine-headed horse.

Two accessories are absolutely necessary for the full-cheek

snaffle, although you do see people riding without them. This bit is designed to have small leather loops called bit keepers that slip over the top points of the branches and through the cheek piece of the bridle, keeping the bit upright. The line of the bit should follow the line of the horse's head. Without these little bit keepers, the bit will tilt until it sits at a 90-degree angle to the horse's head. At this angle the bit is less attractive—and also less effective.

The leather loops also give you the advantage of being able to exert a small amount of poll pressure that is not normally present when using the snaffle. This is useful when giving a preparatory command for a halt or downward transition.

The full-cheek bit sits very evenly in the horse's mouth, and

The details of turnout are important in the show ring, including the full-cheek snaffle with bit keepers that help the rider give preparatory command to the poll.

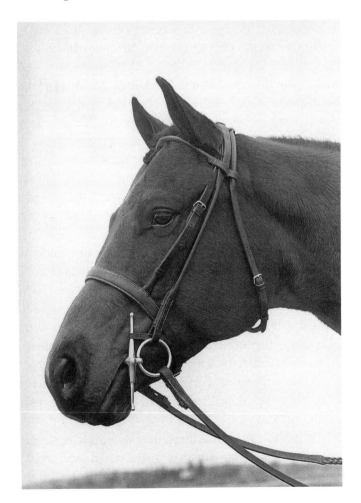

when used for lateral work, it has an effect similar to that of the bosal hackamore. The bit by design puts pressure on the outside of the horse's face and asks the horse to give and soften in the direction of the bend.

Virtually all types of mouthpiece are available with each type of cheek, although you may have to search the catalogs to find the exact combination for your horse. Copper is used in many mouthpieces to encourage the horse to salivate. German silver is also comfortable for the horse to carry, as there is a small amount of copper in the alloy. Sweet iron, which rusts slightly, is also acceptable to the horse; it is used in many better Western bits.

Stainless steel is also frequently used for mouthpieces. In the Western bits, various alloys of silver are used to add a decorative aspect, as well as to contribute to the balance of the bit through the distribution of weight.

Cheap chrome bits are to be avoided. The chrome soon flakes away, leaving little minicraters that irritate the mouth. How would you like spending your days with a piece of your car bumper in your mouth? You can easily recognize chrome, as it has a distinctive shine.

The horse is far happier when the bit glides easily over a coating of saliva. A dry-mouthed, tense horse will sometimes feel the bit "stick" in place, just as when you touch your tongue to an ice cube and everything sticks together. The mouthpiece should remain centered in the horse's mouth, and the horse's head should remain centered on its body, not taken far to one side or the other.

In training, I find that horses with very thick lips need more pressure in the center of their tongue. A horse with thin lips may prefer a bit with more tongue relief.

As I mentioned before, snaffles are used one side at a time to influence that same side of the horse. In contrast, pulling on one rein of a curb or leverage bit will result in pressure throughout the entire bit.

You hear people complain about hardmouthed horses. Actually, hardmouthed horses are horses who are not educated to the bridle. They've learned to stiffen their shoulders, neck, and jaws. Many hardmouthed horses have been reformed and restored to lightness by being reschooled in mild bits that allowed them to seek comfort instead of fear.

Let's say that the guy standing next to you slugs you with a set of brass knuckles. The first time is going to surprise you, and it is going to hurt. When you see that it's going to happen a second time, you tighten up your entire body, especially your neck and shoulder, and prepare for that blow. You probably won't have anything else on your mind except being ready for that painful impact.

An overbitted horse will tighten its body and mind in preparation for the discomfort it anticipates. This will make the horse difficult to train, as its mind won't be fully on your commands, and it certainly won't contribute to an outstanding performance, as the horse will be scared of the bit and won't work with confidence.

The only way to get a horse to stay soft, mobile in the shoulder, and giving in the poll, is to use a comfortable but effective bit that does not violate the horse's trust.

A horse who is trained in the snaffle experiences comfort and relaxation and develops a trust in its rider. The horse will be more forgiving if the rider does make a mistake—and will be much more open to learning.

Curb Bits

When you move on to the curb bit, you have to be lighter still with your hands. You might be able to use a ten-pound pull on the snaffle, but the same pull on the curb bit will inflict a lot of discomfort on the horse because the leverage compounds the effect.

A curb bit is any bit with a shank attached to a mouthpiece and that is used with a strap or chain under the chin. The curb bit affects the horse's poll as well as its bars and beneath its chin (where the curb chain or strap rests). Without that curb strap or chain, the curb bit has only minimal influence on the poll. That is why it is so important to adjust this bit correctly, including the curb strap. All the pieces must have the correct relationship to one another.

If the curb strap is too loose, the bit rotates too much before coming into effect. If the curb strap is too tight, there will be constant pressure under the horse's chin, deadening and chafing the area. The horse will become oversensitive in that spot and be inclined to toss its head in response. The horse will also be less inclined to go forward freely because it is anticipating that discomfort under the chin.

Remember that you have to constantly check the fit of your equipment. Leather curb straps stretch and twist, and must be inspected daily. Curb chains of good width with multiple fine links can be very effective, yet relatively comfortable. They stay adjusted

Shown are various curb bits and their levels of severity rated from #1—the most forgiving—to #10—the most severe.

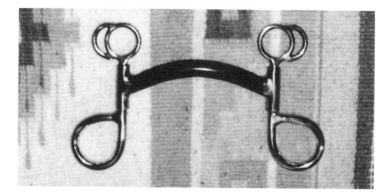

1-to-1-ratio loose-jaw large-sized smooth mullen mouthpiece: #1

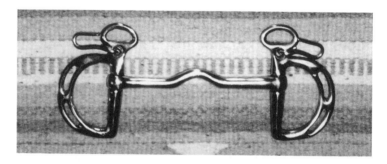

1-to-1-ratio medium-sized smooth kimberwick mouthpiece: #2

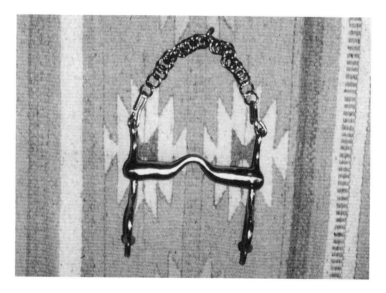

2-to-1-ratio S-shank solid-jaw large-sized smooth mouthpiece with small tongue release: #3

1-to-1-ratio broken-mouth medium-sized wrapped-wire mouthpiece: 3# (used with two hands) or #6 (used with one hand)

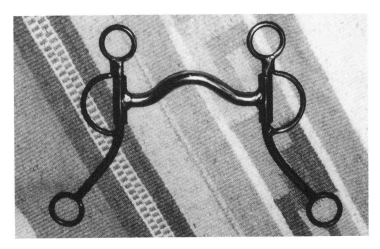

4-to-1-ratio loose-jaw large-sized mouthpiece, wide tongue release: #6

4-to-1-ratio small-sized mouthpiece with wide tongue release: #8

1-to-8-ratio small-mouth mullen bumper bit with solid iron curb strap: #10

just as you position them because they do not stretch. Curb chains with a few large, coarse links are less comfortable for the horse because they are knobbier and rougher.

The curb bit's severity is also affected by the design and texture of the mouthpiece. Thin mouthpieces are more severe than thicker ones. Crickets and rollers can help make a bit more user-friendly to the horse and encourage the horse to relax its jaw and salivate freely.

Various styles and designs of mouthpieces, from frogs to spades, from half-breeds to roller curbs, can contribute to the balance of the bit in the mouth as well as to the comfort of the horse.

To fully understand the refinements in the use of the curb bit, you need to have a full grasp of preparatory commands. The horse must know what to expect from you at all times, and you can help out by sending the horse a little advance notice before you actually perform a movement or exercise. It's like a little minisignal before the bit actually takes effect. Pulling on one rein of the curb bit will influence the entire mouth because the mouthpiece is solid.

Various types of curb bits have different linkages in the mouthpiece and cheekpieces. In general, bits with flexible, hinged cheekpieces (known as loose-jaw bits) are less severe than the stiff grazing bits. A rider using a loose-jaw bit can communicate with his or her horse in a much more refined manner. The flexible bit responds to the slightest movement of the rider's fingers and telegraphs an alert to the horse. In contrast, getting the same effect with a solid bit such as the straight-shanked solid-jaw bit takes much more effort and detracts from the lightness of your horse.

Let's follow the progress of a preparatory command given to a horse in a curb bit. First, the rider decides what he or she is going to do. The rider then signals the horse by a small shift of body weight and a tiny movement of the fingers in the rein hand. That movement is transmitted down the reins to the bit, which moves

The curb chain or strap should be adjusted to lie smoothly in the curb groove with approximately two fingers worth of room between the horse's jaw and the chain.

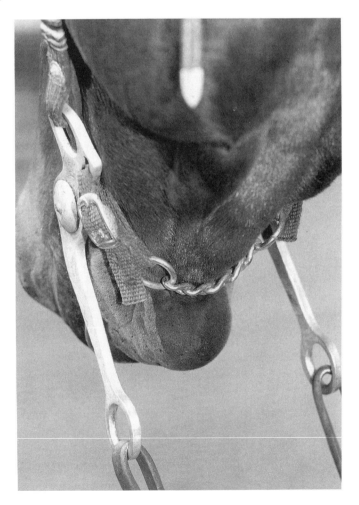

slightly and puts a small pressure on the chin strap. Depending on the type of bit, there may be a small amount of pressure on the center of the tongue as well. The curb bit also places pressure through the bridle on the top of the poll, asking the horse to yield (this is called poll pressure). Finally, the bars under the lips and tongue feel pressure.

High-port bits such as the half-breed or spade will also transmit a small amount of contact to the palate, or to the roof of the mouth. The spade bit is often criticized because it is frequently used by those who have neither the skill or the patience to use such a delicate means of communication. If the bit is fitted correctly and used skillfully, this bit can become the tool of a master. A hammer can smash rocks or it can work together with a chisel and make a beautiful sculpture. It's not the hammer's fault that it is capable of smashing things.

Curb bits vary in severity, both in mouthpiece design, and in the length of the shank, or lever. There is leverage both below the mouthpiece and above. Remember that Archimedes said he could move the world with a lever if only he had a place to stand. That gives you an idea of the potential strength given to you by the curb bit, a lever in itself; this lever can influence the horse for better or worse.

If there is a three-inch shank below the mouthpiece, and a one-inch shank above, that is a three-to-one ratio. Put a ten-pound pull on that three-to-one ratio and you have thirty pounds of pull on the horse's mouth. If we move to a four-to-one ratio, we're looking at forty pounds of pressure with that ten pound pull, and with a five-to-one ratio, it's fifty pounds.

In the show ring, Western horses older than five years old are expected to show in the curb bit with only one hand on the reins. That is one of the reasons riders ultimately move into the curb bit. A well-trained Western horse performing with lightness in a curb bit can be a pleasure to watch.

Bosal Hackamores

The bosal hackamore is a bitless rawhide training device that exerts pressure on the horse's nose and jaw. It is a master's tool for training. (I refer only to the bosal when I used the word "hackamore"; the mechanical hackamore is not suited for the

Pencil bosal   **12-plait 5/8 inch bosal**   **6-plait 1-inch bosal**

training of horses, but can be used effectively in speed events and trail riding.)

A good bosal is a work of art because it is hand braided of rawhide. The more plaits, the better the quality, and the better the bosal is for your horse. Bosals made of few plaits, such as six, tend to be coarser and more likely to skin your horse up. In contrast, the multiple-strand bosals, such as the sixteen-strand type, are much smoother and reflect the craftsmanship that went into their making. The tighter the braid, the finer the braid. The beveled edges of good rawhide work are much more comfortable to the horse and will give the horse a feel rather than a bite when you take up contact.

Only a rawhide-cored bosal is acceptable in the show ring and for serious training. A cable-cored bosal cannot be shaped properly, as it will always return to the neutral shape dictated by the cable core.

The bosal must be shaped like a pear so that it falls away from the horse's chin. If the bosal is wedge shaped, as are all cable-cored bosals, it will bark the horse's hair and tend to pinch the horse. New bosals often must be shaped. You can use a coffee can to get a good shape: slip the dampened bosal over the can and tie it in place with the mecate rope knot.

A good hackamore horse won't last if you make him sore. It used to be popular to skin the horse up a little, especially on the bridge of the nose; however, this is not effective. If you've got a sore hand and some guy comes up and wants to give you a power handshake, you're going to draw back and tighten up your whole body, anticipating the discomfort. The same holds true for the horse who anticipates being hurt. The old-timers always felt that a sore horse was going to stop where you wanted, but I've had more runaways with a sore-chinned horse than I've ever had with a light, unmarked horse. If you see that your bosal is starting to mark the hair over the bridge of your horse's nose, or under its chin, grease those areas with petroleum jelly and, if necessary, pad the rough areas on the bosal with electrical tape.

Position the bosal on the bridge of your horse's nose, right where the skull bones end and the cartilage begins. You can easily feel that area when you run your fingers along the front of the horse's head. The heel knot should hang down away from the chin bones and close to the horse's lower lip when there is no pressure on the reins. Be careful not to position the knot too tightly. The skin is very thin over the lower jaw, and it is easy to sore a horse in this area, particularly if you are using a horsehair mecate.

Many riders are having success using soft rope mecates. Although the prickly horsehair does play a role in causing a horse to back off the bridle, we aren't dealing with the same kind of horses today that our grandfathers were buckarooing. A responsive horse will work with softer aids.

A fiador (also called a Theodore by some cowboys) is knotted to the bosal to serve as a throatlatch and prevent the heel knot from ever being pulled off of the horse's chin. If you are leading a horse with a bosal, use the mecate lead rope and knot the reins with a half hitch over the poll if you don't have a fiador. Otherwise the horse could pull back for a second and shuck the bosal and bridle right off of its head.

The bosal influences the horse's nose, chin, and poll, and there are two preparatory commands involved in using it: picking up the mecate and squeezing the hand. The horse will feel a little pressure on the nose and on the poll before the heel knot comes into contact with its chin, and for a light, well-schooled horse, that is all that is needed. The bosal is always used with two hands, but you never pull back with both hands at the same time. You use one hand or the other, but not both.

The classic Western horse is generally started in a large, thick bosal, as much as an inch in diameter. As the horse's training progresses, smaller and thinner bosals are used. (The severity of a bosal is determined by its thickness and whether or not the braid edges are beveled smooth, or rough and abrasive.) The horse is penultimately ridden in both a pencil bosal and a curb bit at the same time. A skilled rider can handle all four reins and initiate commands on the bosal first so that the horse is prepared for the use of the bit. Later, the horse is weaned to work only off of the bit.

This is the classic method of finishing the training of the Western horse, schooling first with both bosal and curb, then gradually weaning the horse to work only off of the bit.

This process is an entire book in itself, and few trainers care to take this amount of time anymore. You do see a few mature horses ridden in bosals, often because they display problems with the bit or because they are quiet and light in the bosal.

A bosal is also useful in reschooling racehorses, and in getting three- and four-year-old horses through those stages when they are shedding the caps of their teeth. When horses are teething, their mouth is sore, and the bosal enables you to go on with your training without hurting them.

Side-Pulls

Side-pulls are a fairly recent innovation. Plain side-pulls have just a strap over the horse's nose, and only influence the horse in one way; with pressure on the bridge of the nose. Frankly, this is just like riding in a tight halter.

There are also side-pulls with various snaffle mouthpieces, and these do offer you a combination effect, but lack the sophistication of the bosal and snaffle. The texture and size of the noseband can also be modified to increase the severity of the side-pull. Some are plain leather; others are one or two strands of hard-twist lariat that can really bark up a nose. The result of the harsher nosebands is that the horse flinches every time it feels you start to give a command; you can't get anywhere in this situation.

A sensitive horse will give you lateral bending in the side-pull. You just have to experiment sometimes to see what tack a horse will respond to best.

Selecting the Right Bitting

I look at bitting the way some people shop for sound systems. If I walk into the store and buy a cheap portable radio, I've got something that turns on and off and picks up the local stations, but doesn't do a lot more. The same applies to a snaffle bit: I can use it to do the basics but it takes a lot of skill to go beyond the basics with a snaffle.

If I walk into the store and decide I want something a notch better, I'll probably get a stereo system of some kind. Now I've got multiple speakers and sophisticated adjustment of the bass and

The side-pull is a useful schooling tool for the green horse.

treble modes. That's the way I see the bosal hackamore. It is more sophisticated than the snaffle. I have nose and poll pressure, and I can refine my training to a degree. My "stereo" goes off, on, and adjusts.

Now I'm ready to really step up to the top of the line, and I buy a whole home-entertainment system. I can do anything I want to in this setup, and that's the way the curb bit works. I have preparatory commands in the poll, the chin, and the palate, and I can really lighten a horse while doing sophisticated work like lead changes, sliding stops, and spins.

Of course, you always have Cousin Leo diddling with your fine home-entertainment system, and after he's gone, you find that the sound is all out of whack and the speakers sound like they're sitting in the bottom of a trash can. You have to use your educated hand to get everything back in synch again. The same thing happens to the horse in the curb bit because the world is full of Cousin Leos. A rider who neglects to give preparatory commands, or who uses no other aids except for a yank on the reins, will quickly cause the horse's training to regress to an elementary level.

When the vaqueros were training their fine bridle horses on the ranch, they were careful about who rode those horses. A good horse could be ruined in a single day by an unskilled or unsympathetic rider, and the remudas were usually full of horses like that. The best, most responsive horses were kept in private strings and out of the hands of the general public.

**One pair of good hands is better
than having a thousand bits.**

22

❀　❀　❀

A Good Saddle
Is an Investment

You can't go wrong if you buy the best possible saddle you can afford. An ill-fitting or poorly designed saddle is like a pebble in your shoe—it will always be a distraction and make you and your horse uncomfortable.

Features to Consider

Riders can handicap themselves by buying a cheap, flashy saddle that was either designed for another sport or made strictly for the dude-ranch set. A surprising number of stock saddles are designed with the fenders hung a little forward to encourage a rider to take a chair seat. While these saddles are comfortable, they are not at all suited for athletic horsemanship.

In any saddle, English or Western, you want the sweet spot, or the spot where you will naturally sit, to be right over the stirrups. The fenders and leathers should be right under the sweet spot so that it is easy for you to keep your legs under you. If your legs are right under your body, you are in balance and able to give controlled, delicate commands with only the slightest movement of your muscles. When your legs are correctly placed, you will have full use of your lower leg and it will be at a correct angle.

Remember, if you look down and can see your toe, that means you are in a chair seat. Hide your toes underneath your knees. If the horse vanishes in a puff of smoke, you should still be able to stand on your feet.

Top-quality leather is essential in a saddle. I prefer to buy my saddles with light-colored leather. You can always darken a saddle later, or let it weather naturally. The reason for buying a light-colored saddle to begin with is to get the best possible leather. Only the best hides are suitable for use in natural-colored saddlery—

This is an example of what I like to see in a Western saddle. Notice the higher cantle and the placement of the lowest point of the seat. The stirrup placement gives the rider maximum balance. The higher cantle gives extra support. This is a Richard Shrake Resistance-Free Saddle made by Circle Y.

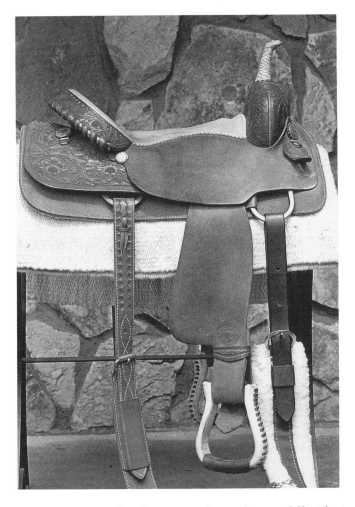

This is a good example of a flat-seated cutting saddle that gives the rider a lot of freedom of movement—which can be good or bad.

those without scars, uneven spots, or other mars. In contrast, dark dye or heavy oiling (which isn't good for leather) can hide a lot of cosmetic defects, and this treatment isn't the best way to take care of your gear.

I like to see thin leather fenders on a Western saddle. A lot of stock saddles have thick fenders that don't take a shape easily and don't allow you to communicate well with the horse. Riding in such a saddle is like playing piano while wearing oven mitts. Thin fenders let you use your legs to greater effect and keep your aids light.

A monel or other heavy stirrup gives the rider more stability because a heavy stirrup doesn't swing around as much. It works as a counterbalance. Heavy stirrups are especially helpful for the English rider. A Fillis-type iron is much easier to pick up and keep on the foot than the cheap, chrome irons often found on inexpensive saddles.

I want to see a higher-than-usual cantle on my Western saddles. There was a fad for a while in the sixties and seventies for a low, rolled cantle. A lazy rider would end up right on top of this low cantle, and the cantle would just about disappear. The low cantle encouraged riders to park their weight too far back, causing them to bounce on top of their horse's kidneys all the time. The higher cantle doesn't let you slip out of the sweet spot so easily.

There is a trend at the moment for a very flat seat. I don't particularly like a flat seat. If race-car drivers used standard bench seats in their speed machines, they'd be sliding all over the place on those fast turns. That's why they prefer a bucket seat. I'm not advocating an extreme seat like the old "bear traps" or even the equitation saddles that practically held you in place with built-up fronts. I just like to see a saddle with a moderately shaped sweet spot that is easy to find and with a little bit of pocket on the sides for your legs. That pocket helps keep your legs steady and more stable.

A rider who is floating all over an uncooperative saddle will be constantly changing his or her equilibrium, and constantly trying to catch up with the horse. Or the horse will be struggling to figure out just what all those squeezes and tugs mean. The idea is to be locked into one performing unit, and you can't do that if you're all over your horse's back.

The rigging I like to see on my Western saddles is close to being a center-fire setting. I want to see the rigging set in the skirt instead of in the tree because it will set lower and be more stable on the horse's back. Tree rigging is often seen in those little barrel-racing saddles that perch on the horse's spine like a peanut on a snake. They move around a lot unless they're cinched up tight enough to cut the horse in two. A lot of friction and heat builds up underneath them.

Your rigging must distribute pressure throughout the entire saddle, not concentrate pressure over the horse's shoulders. Think of wearing high-heeled shoes—all your weight is on the toes and ball of your foot. You're a lot happier in running shoes, where your weight is evenly distributed throughout the foot. The same applies to the horse.

While center-fire riggings work very well on many horses, there are short-withered horses who work better in a three-quarter rigging. It depends on the individual.

The cinch on your saddle should be of good quality and wide. Wide cinches grip the horse better and are more comfortable. If you don't believe that, try tying a piece of clothesline around your waist as tightly as you can, then doing the same with a wide leather belt.

Tooling and stamping can make leather wear longer because the density of the leather is increased where it is stamped down, and the wear is directed at the raised areas. It's the same idea as sculptured shag carpet. In my collection of antique saddles, I notice that the tooled saddles have stood up best to the test of time and use. Tooling can also increase the flexibility of the leather and give the rider a little more traction.

Trying Out a Saddle

When you try a saddle out, use a sheet of newspaper for a pad and ride for a while. Get the horse hot. Then pull off the saddle and see what the paper looks like. Are there any tears or spots where it is rubbed through? Those signify pressure points that will cause you problems in the long run. Ideally, the entire paper should be dampened evenly, showing you that the saddle fits uniformly over the entire back. If there are dry spots, those may indicate places where there is so much pressure that the horse's sweat glands are literally unable to function.

If the saddle isn't comfortable enough for a short ride with a newspaper for a pad, it isn't going to suit the horse for long days, even with the fanciest or thickest pad you can find. The more you pad a saddle, the higher it sits off the horse's back, and the more unstable you will be.

If you are trying out a used saddle, look at the sheepskin underneath. If there are bald patches, those may be pressure points that will affect your horse. The wear on the sheepskin should be uniform.

Check that the tree is sound by placing your knee in the seat, grasping the horn and the cantle, and pulling firmly. Obviously the saddle that folds in half during this treatment isn't the one you want. Be sure as well that the tree is centered in the saddle. Some saddles are one-sided from the very start because of sloppy design or construction. If your saddle isn't balanced, you will never be balanced yourself.

Buying a saddle is just like buying a car. The cheaper one won't have all the amenities that you'd like to have—and will probably not wear as well either. If worse comes to worst, you can always resell a top-quality saddle and get most if not all of your money out of it. Try doing that with a piece of junk.

English Saddles

In English saddles, buy the very best you can afford. In general, the European-made saddles are of the best quality. Avoid the saddles from Argentina and India. These cheap saddles often pinch the horse's back because they are badly designed. You cannot ride well on a saddle that is poorly made.

It is extremely important to fit an English saddle correctly to the individual horse because the trees are very flexible under the weight of a rider, which can result in pinching. You will notice a difference in the position of an English saddle before and after you mount.

The principles in fitting an English saddle are essentially the same as with the stock saddle. There should be no pressure on the horse's spine, and the saddle should fit smoothly over the horse's back and ribs without gapping or excessive pressure. Again, the newspaper test can be helpful.

The pads used with jumping and dressage saddles are a lot thinner than those used under stock saddles, so the fit of the saddle is much more crucial. English saddles also don't distribute the rider's weight as much over the horse's back and ribs as the stock saddle does with its wide skirts.

The English saddle, whether it be a cutback, a dressage, or a jumping saddle, should have the pommel and the top of the cantle at approximately the same level. If the pommel rests dramatically higher, that is a good clue that the saddle is too narrow for that horse. Many people fix such problems with the use of lollipop or wedge pads to raise the cantle; however, this should not be done if the difference in pommel and cantle heights is more than slight. Lollipop and wedge pads change the weight distribution, and if the saddle is too narrow, the horse will feel that tree being rammed right into its shoulders at every step. It's better to experiment with a wider tree and perhaps a slight wedge pad for the sake of the horse.

A tree that is too wide is easier to fix than one that is too narrow. You can always pad up a big saddle, but it's hard to do much about one that's too small. Be careful, however. Excess padding on an English saddle results in a saddle that sits too far off of the horse's back, losing stability from side to side. If the horse is low-withered as well, you can just about spin the saddle like a top, no matter how tight the girth may be.

An English saddle that is properly fitted doesn't need a girth to hold it in place once the rider is mounted. Now that doesn't mean we should all leave our girths at home, but it does mean that we shouldn't be strapping the girth until the horse's eyes are bulging. The girth helps keep the saddle from moving excessively on the horse's back, as well as keeping it in place during mounting and dismounting.

The English saddle should not interfere with the movement of the horse's shoulder blades. For some reason, a lot of people want to put their jumping saddles right on top of the horse's shoulder blades. This is not only uncomfortable for the horse, but results in an out-of-balance rider.

The Fit of the Saddle

In all saddles, there is an area where the saddle rests comfortably on the horse's back, provided the saddle fits reasonably well. Place the saddle slightly ahead of where it belongs and rock it gently back into a position where it seems to be at home. When it settles and stabilizes, notice where that is in relation to the horse's shoulder blades and heart girth. The girth or cinch on either type of saddle should not be right in the horse's armpit, but about a hand's breadth behind that area, depending on the conformation of the horse and the type of rigging on the saddle.

There is a wide variety of pads available to absorb shock and make horses more comfortable, and many minor problems can be worked out by adjusting the padding. In addition, English saddles can be restuffed to some degree to make up for minor problems in fit.

The reason I emphasize the quality and fit of saddles and tack is that the horse cannot be in a resistance-free state if the horse is uncomfortable with its equipment. If you spend your day at work sitting in an ill-fitting chair, you may have an idea what your horse goes through with a saddle that isn't quite right.

For the show ring and for good general maintenance, you want to keep your saddle clean and well cared for. You must also keep cinches, girths, and pads clean for the comfort of the horse and to make them last longer. If your horse is sore from dirty or ill-fitting tack, the horse isn't going to do its job.

Glossary

✿   ✿   ✿

Above the Bit: The horse who is above the bit is in an inverted frame with its head held higher than the withers. This frame is common with horses who are ewe-necked or who have been badly ridden for a long period of time. The horse's back will be hollow, and its hocks typically will trail out behind the body. The withers are not "up," but dropped. The rider seems astraddle a drooping suspension bridge. Horses in this posture are typically tense and respond to cues by further hollowing their backs. The front line of the horse's face is typically pointed outward, rather than vertical, and in extreme cases, the horse may resemble an alligator, with its head held horizontally.

Balanced Seat: Also known as the dressage seat, the balanced seat has a lot in common with the correctly ridden stock seat. The rider is in an upright posture with full contact in the saddle at all times except in the posting trot. The balanced seat can be used in combination with the forward seat for jumping and cross-country riding.

Behind the Bit: The horse who is behind the bit typically curves its neck at the third vertebra of the neck instead of at the first vertebra immediately behind the poll. The front line of the face is not vertical, but tilted inward, toward the horse's chest. Contact with the bit is often minimal, as these horses coil themselves into a posture that comes right up to the bit but never takes an honest contact. Horses with this fault can be more difficult to correct than those who are above the bit because it is a more subtle fault, and the inexperienced rider is often fooled into thinking that it is correct because the horse is not showing active rebellion. Horses who are behind the bit are not going forward correctly. This fault is extremely common in horses who have been forced into position by the use of draw reins.

Bosal: A bosal is a shaped noseband of braided leather that is often used in the early training of the horse. Green horses are started in thick bosals, and the size of the bosal is gradually reduced as the horse progresses in his education. On a true bosal, there are no metal parts at all. The bosal works by applying pressure to the poll, the bridge of the nose, and the chin.

Cadence: Cadence refers to the rhythm of the horse's footfalls. The horse is moving actively, yet precisely and correctly in perfect rhythm. Cadence can make a good horse become a brilliant horse. Although it can be difficult to explain cadence, it is easy to recognize it. Horses with cadence draw your eye to their excellence.

Center: Your center is located just above and within the cage of your pelvis. It is the location of your center of gravity and is the "heart" of your body as far as physical activity is concerned. Do not confuse your center with your belly button. If you went inward several inches from your belly button to the central core of your body, you would be at your center.

Center of Gravity: A person's center of gravity is a dynamic point that is always changing with the motion of the horse or person. It is a point of balance that shifts according to momentum and posture. When you are standing, your center and your center of gravity coincide. When you are sprinting in the one hundred-yard dash, your center of gravity is moving forward and upward into your trunk to a point where all forces are in balance. If your center of gravity gets too far forward, you will fall on your face.

Chocolate Side: This is a German expression referring to the strong or good side of a rider. Your chocolate side is the one where everything is easy. While most riders have a chocolate side, top-class riders develop both sides of their body to be equally skilled.

Cow: Cow is that quality shown by a horse who expresses an interest in working or playing with cattle. In truth, a horse with cow will work anything, from children to chickens, as that horse has an instinctive response to movement. In top horses, cow is also shown in their ability to read an animal and anticipate which way it will move next.

Curb Bit: A curb bit is a bit with leverage that applies pressure on the poll, the chin groove, and the bars of the mouth. Any bit that does not have a direct line of connection between your hand and the bit is typically a curb bit. The severity of a curb bit is determined by the length of the shanks and the ratio of the part below the mouthpiece to the part above. A curb bit can be loose-jaw, with hinged shanks that move, or rigid, as in the grazing-type bits that do not have any points of movement in the bit itself. There are many different mouthpieces available in curb bits for all different horse sports.

Diaphragm: The diaphragm is the muscular and tendinous partition between the chest and the abdomen. It is the internal mechanism that expands and contracts to regulate breathing. It's also the place where you get hiccups. It is located just above the center of your body.

Dressage: Dressage means training. It also refers to a popular horse sport that is one of the three classical sports, the other two being show jumping and three-day eventing. Dressage is based on the classical methods of horse training that date back to the ancient Greeks, who first used dressage to prepare their cavalry horses.

Fiador: The fiador is a knotted cord that forms a throatlatch and an additional point of attachment for a bosal. It prevents the bosal from being pulled off of the horse's chin if you are leading the horse with both the reins and the lead end of the mecate. The fiador is sometimes called a Theodore (often by the same people who call a mecate a McCarty).

Forward Seat: The forward seat is the style of riding used for jumping. The father of hunt-seat equitation, the forward seat was developed in its modern form by Federico Caprilli, who amply demonstrated that his then-unique position was much better suited than the balanced seat for jumping obstacles and going fast cross country.

Half-Halt: The half-halt is a dressage term referring to the momentary rebalancing and preparation of the horse before performing a maneuver or transition. It can also be described as a preparatory command.

Hunt Seat: Hunt seat refers to a style of horsemanship derived from the cavalry methods, oriented toward riding on the flat and jumping. It is one of three types of English riding. Hunt-seat riders position their upper body slightly forward in order to follow the horse's center of gravity while jumping and riding fast cross country.

In the Bridle: A horse who is in the bridle is actively engaged behind and carries its back and withers in an upward posture, like a suspension bridge that slightly arched up. The head is vertical, and the horse carries the bit with the appropriate contact for the style of riding and the type of bit. The horse's movement is elastic and lively, with a true cadence and springiness that makes the horse light and pleasurable to watch. The horse is alert for any maneuver and is totally without resistance throughout its body and mind.

Jigging: Jigging is an unpleasant, choppy trot a horse makes when it won't walk quietly. This gait does not get you anywhere except annoyed. It is a sign of bad behavior and becomes quite uncomfortable for the rider after a while. It is only acceptable in the case of the speed-event horse who is so anticipating its run that it is pretuning its body to fly.

Leaking: Leaking refers to the action of a cutting horse moving slowly away from the herd area as the horse works a cow. The horse is termed to be literally "leaking" out of position and placing himself in a bad position for the next cow.

Mecate: Traditionally the bosal is used with a braided-horsehair rope called a mecate or McCarty. The mecate is attached under the bosal in a chin knot, then leads like two reins to the rider's hand. This rope is extremely prickly, and riders using it usually wear gloves. The prickliness of the rope helps back the horse off the bosal. When a rider lifts the mecate slightly in a preparatory command, the light prickle warns the horse of the upcoming transition before the knot hits its chin.

Mullen Mouth: The mullen mouth is a bit that is found in dozens of configurations in both curb and snaffle designs. It is shaped like a half-moon and is very comfortable for the horse. It is especially common in pelham bits, and can be found in Western styles. It offers tongue relief without any hint of a nutcracker effect. The mullen mouth is a particularly good bit for horses with cut tongues.

Narrow Eyes: If you have narrow eyes you have a narrow fixed focus on one point, often your horse's ears, and you become stiff and quite unaware of your surroundings. A person who is totally focused in narrow eyes can be surrounded by the entire White House staff in punk haircuts without knowing it.

Nutcracker Effect: The nutcracker effect refers to the action of center-jointed or "broken" bits, which close tightly around the horse's lower jaw, like a nutcracker. The center joint of these bits often pokes up into the horse's palate as well.

On the Bit: A horse who is on the bit is in an active and lively posture that enables the horse to perform any maneuver if given the appropriate preparatory commands. As opposed to a horse who is in the bridle, a horse on the bit may be in a more upright posture, with its head and neck held higher, but continuing to show a correct shape and arch of the neck. The back and withers are arched, and the horse carries more of its weight on its hind legs than on its front legs. The horse is well engaged behind in order to support more of its body weight on the hind legs, making its forehand mobile and light. If the reins are loosened on a horse who is on the bit, the horse falls apart; the horse who is in the bridle maintains its frame on a slack rein. Racehorses, driving horses, and hunters traditionally are ridden on the bit.

Open Eyes: A rider with open eyes shows complete and total awareness of his or her surroundings and the activities going on therein. When using open eyes, the rider automatically adopts a more relaxed but correct posture, ready and able to utilize the feedback from the eyes.

Preparatory Commands: Preparatory commands are subtle warning cues that instruct the horse to adjust its balance and position in order to be ready for an action or transition. They are like the yellow warning light before a red light, the words "get ready, get set" before the word "go." (See also Half-halt.)

Resistance-free Horsemanship: Resistance-free horsemanship is the result of a horse and rider working in complete harmony and unity, with no resistance in body or mind of either. It is our goal, no matter what horse sport we perform.

Rhythm: Rhythm refers to the sequence and consistency of the footfalls of the horse. For example, a horse who is four-beating at the canter is showing an impure rhythm. It would be impossible for a four-beater to show cadence. A limping horse would also be unable to show correct rhythm or cadence.

Ripple Effect: The ripple effect is the rebound of the horse's movement from the ground. If you stamp your foot hard on firm ground, you will feel the impact throughout your body. In a more subtle sense, the ripple effect utilizes that rebound to enhance and create brilliance in the horse's performance. For the rider, it entails the ability to know what is happening with the horse's body and feet without having to look, influencing the horse as necessary with correct cues that restore and maintain ideal movement. Each time the horse's foot strikes the ground, the rider feels the ripple effect.

Romal Reins: Romal reins are part of the vaquero tradition of horsemanship. They are generally made of braided leather with buttons added to create a perfectly balanced unit with a spade or half-breed bit, and they have a long attachment known as the romal at the end of the closed rein. The romal, a whiplike braided quirt, may be used to encourage cattle or sluggish horses. Romal reins are held in an ice-cream-cone position coming up from the bottom of the hand.

Rubbernecking: The horse who rubbernecks is quite capable of looking south while the rest of its body goes west. The rider has lost control of the horse's shoulders, and the horse is "spilling out" through that opening and proceeding as it wishes, while seeming to comply to the rider's command with its head. A rubbernecker will give in the neck but not in the body, so the horse's bend is incorrect. A horse that rubber-necks can be corrected by keeping its outside shoulder under control.

Saddle Seat: Saddle seat is a style of horsemanship designed to showcase gaited breeds such as the American saddlebred and the Tennessee walking horse. It is also a popular riding style in breeds such as the Morgan, the Arabian, and occasionally, the Appaloosa.

Snaffle Bit: The snaffle bit is any bit that gives you a direct contact from your hands to the mouthpiece; in other words, a bit that does not have leverage. It influences the horse strictly through pressure on the bars of the mouth and the tongue. It can be a tool of finesse, or a means of cruelty in the wrong hands.

Spade Bit: The spade bit is a curb bit with a high port or spoon for the horse who is completely finished in its training and has a rider with educated hands. It is an extremely light bit that communicates the most subtle cues to the horse; however, it can be abused in the wrong hands. When a rider lifts the reins slightly in a preparatory command for a transition, the high port or spoon gives a warning tap on the horse's palate before the horse feels the leverage effect from the chinstrap on its jaw.

Split Reins: Split reins are common to the Texas style of Western horsemanship. There is no point of attachment between the two reins. They may be held in the same fashion as the romal reins, like an ice cream cone with the reins coming up from the bottom of the hand, or with a flatter "hand shake" position with the reins coming in through the top of a single hand.

Stock Seat: Stock seat is the formal term for Western horseman-ship. It derives its name from originally being the practical and comfortable horsemanship of the cowboy and vaquero. Most open or AHSA-approved shows use the term for western equitation classes; breed shows use the term *Western horsemanship*.

Sweet Spot: The sweet spot is the place in the saddle where you are naturally inclined to sit. In a well-designed saddle, this will be in a place that encourages and allows good riding position. In poorly designed saddles, the sweet spot may be placed in such a manner as to encourage you to sit badly, or make you unable to go with the movement of the horse.

Tempo: Tempo is the rate of the speed of the horse's striding or footfalls. It does not necessarily have anything to do with speed of the horse. A horse can have a fast tempo but still be taking short strides, as is seen in the racking American saddlebred. The Western horse typically has a relaxed tempo with a balanced stride.

Transition: A transition is the act of changing from one gait or movement to the next. A transition can be made roughly and abruptly, or it can be a smooth action that flows without interruption.

Index

❀ ❀ ❀